CHRISTIAN ROMAN EMPIRE SERIES

Vol. 8

THE

LIFE

OF THE

BLESSED EMPEROR
CONSTANTINE

FROM AD 306 TO AD 337

by
Eusebius Pamphilus

Evolution Publishing
Merchantville NJ
2009

Originally Published by
Samuel Bagster and Sons, London
1845

This edition ©2009 by Evolution Publishing
Merchantville, New Jersey.

Printed in the United States of America

ISBN 978-1-889758-93-0

Library of Congress Cataloging-in-Publication Data

Eusebius, of Caesarea, Bishop of Caesarea, ca. 260-ca. 340.
  [Life of Constantine]
  The life of the Blessed Emperor Constantine : from AD 306 to AD 337 /
by Eusebius Pamphilus.
     p. cm. -- (Christian Roman Empire series ; v. 8)
  Originally published: London : Samuel Bagster and Sons, 1845.
  Includes bibliographical references and index.
  ISBN 978-1-889758-93-0
  1. Constantine I, Emperor of Rome, d. 337--Early works to 1800. 2. Emperors
--Rome--Biography--Early works to 1800. 3. Rome--History--Constantine I, the
Great, 306-337--Early works to 1800. I. Title.
  DG315.E9 2009
  937'.08092--dc22
  [B]
                                  2009034613

TABLE OF CONTENTS
TO THE 2009 EDITION

PREFACE TO THE 2009 EDITION

The emperor Constantine the Great is one of those rare figures from antiquity who was tremendously polarizing in his own time, and remains so to this day. Both then and now, he was lauded as a saint, derided as a heretic, cheered as a military hero, criticized as a hypocrite, numbered among the Apostles, and damned as one whose ill-conceived innovations ultimately ruined an empire and corrupted Christianity.

The purpose of this volume is not to dispute any of these notions directly. Instead, we place before the reader an admittedly biased, fulsome, and incomplete biography of Constantine written by a man who knew him well— Eusebius Pamphilus, bishop of Cæsarea. But for all its flaws, Eusebius's *Life of the Blessed Emperor Constantine* is without question the most detailed and intimate portrait of the emperor that has come down to us from antiquity. It is also the sole source for the most important event of Constantine's life—his famous vision of a cross in the sky with the words "Conquer by this."

Though flagrantly effusive in his praise, Eusebius himself was no mean scholar. He was, in fact, one of the most learned and prolific men of his day and can claim credit as the progenitor of the entire field of Church history. And though his biography can be maddeningly vague regarding certain aspects of Constantine's life that intrigue modern scholars, he has done posterity a great service by preserving a multitude of anecdotes about the emperor that appear nowhere else, along with several Constantinian edicts and personal letters included within the body of his biography.

As a panegyric, Eusebius's *Life of Constantine* leaves a great many holes in Constantine's life that may be filled, for better or worse, by other contemporary sources. Accounts of Constantine's life and acts may be found among the works of Eutropius, Aurelius Victor, Lactantius, Socrates, Sozomen, a multitude of panegyricists, and many others. A hostile account may be found in the *New History* of Zosimus, written a little over a century after the emperor's death. So counterpoints do exist to the unremitting praise offered by Eusebius, and these sources should certainly be consulted if one wishes to form a more complete image of Constantine.

This anonymous translation of *The Life of the Blessed Emperor Constantine* was originally published by Samuel Bagster and Sons in 1845. The original introduction to the Bagster edition was a mere two page statement of opinion bereft of any historical value. This has been omitted in this edition. Instead, to help put the *Life* into its historical context, we have added a brief but lucid biography of Eusebius excerpted almost entirely from *A Dictionary of Christian Biography, Literature, Sects and Doctrines* (1880). It is hoped that this introduction will better complement the translation and give the reader an idea of Eusebius's mind, personal history, and motives.

Conversely, as the present work is a biography of sorts in its own right, we have not deemed it necessary to include a capsule biography of Constantine from a more modern perspective in the introduction. Recognizing, however, that Eusebius omitted many episodes that would put his subject in a bad light, we have attempted to remedy this shortcoming with the addition of notes where appropriate.

Finally, the chapter headings contained in this volume were not part of the original *Life* as written by Eusebius but were added by an unknown copyist early in the work's life.[1] As they were included in the Bagster edition, we have largely retained them here, except for those which divided up in a particularly intrusive and artificial way the various Constantinian edicts scattered throughout the *Life*. A curious reader who wishes to find these headers listed in full is encouraged to consult the fine modern translation of the *Life of Constantine* executed by Averil Cameron and Stuart Hall (1999) as part of the Clarendon Ancient History series published by Oxford University Press. This work also includes an impressive amount of commentary and should be sought out by anyone seeking a more detailed and scholarly study of the text.

—*Anthony P. Schiavo, Jr.*
Merchantville, NJ
July 2009

NOTES

1.   See Cameron, p. 54–66.

2009 EDITION BIBLIOGRAPHY AND FURTHER READING

Aurelius Victor. H. W. Bird (transl.) 1994. *De Caesaribus.* Liverpool University Press: Liverpool, UK.

Baker, G. P. 1967. *Constantine the Great and the Christian Revolution.* Barnes and Noble: New York.

Barnes, Timothy D. 1981. *Constantine and Eusebius.* Harvard University Press: Cambridge, MA.

Burckhardt, Jacob. Moses Hadas (transl.) 1949. *The Age of Constantine the Great.* Dorset Books: New York.

Eusebius. Averil Cameron and Stuart G. Hall 1999. *Eusebius: Life of Constantine: Introduction, Translation, and Commentary.* Clarendon Press: Oxford, UK

Eusebius. G. A. Williamson (transl.) 1965. *The History of the Church.* Penguin Books: London.

Eutropius. H. W. Bird (transl.) 1993. *Breviarum ab Urbe Condita of Eutropius.* Liverpool University Press: Liverpool, UK.

Ferguson, Everett et al. (eds.) 1998. *Encyclopedia of Early Christianity.* Garland Publishing: New York.

Gibbon, Edward. 1914. *The History of the Decline and Fall of the Roman Empire.* The MacMillan Company: New York.

Grant, Michael. 1993. *Constantine the Great: The Man and His Times.* Charles Scribner's Sons: New York.

Herbermann, Charles G., et al. 1913. *The Catholic Encyclopedia: An International Work of Reference on the Constitution, Doctrine, Discipline, and History of the Catholic Church.* The Encyclopedia Press: New York. Electronic edition available online at http://www.newadvent.org/cathen/

Julian. Wilmer Cave Wright (transl.) 1969. *The Works of the Emperor Julian.* Volume 2. Harvard University Press: Cambridge, MA.

Lactantius. J. L. Creed (transl.) 1984. *De Mortibus Persecutorum.* Clarendon Press: Oxford, UK.

Lenski, Noel (ed.) 2006. *The Cambridge Companion to the Age of Constantine.* Cambridge University Press: Cambridge, UK.

Lieu, Samuel N. C. and Dominic Montserrat. 1996. *From Constantine to Julian.* Routledge: New York. Includes an English translation of the *Origo Constantini Imperatoris.*

Loomis, Louise Ropes (transl.) 2006. *The Book of the Popes (Liber Pontificalis)* Evolution Publishing: Merchantville, NJ.

Odahl, Charles Matson. 2004. *Constantine and the Christian Empire.* Routledge: London.

Smith, John Holland. 1971. *Constantine the Great.* Charles Scribner's Sons: New York.

Smith, William and Henry Wace. 1880. *A Dictionary of Christian Biography, Literature, Sects and Doctrines.* Volume 2. Little, Brown and Company: Boston.

Socrates. 1874. *The Ecclesiastical History of Socrates.* George Bell and Sons: London.

Sozomen. Edward Walford (transl.) 1855. *The Ecclesiastical History of Sozomen.* Henry G. Bohn: London.

Zosimus. 1814. *New History.* Green and Chaplin: London. Accessed online at: http://www.tertullian.org/fathers/zosimus00_preface.htm

INTRODUCTION

A BRIEF BIOGRAPHY OF EUSEBIUS OF CÆSAREA

Of the date of Eusebius's birth we have no precise information, but the references in his own works enable us to fix it approximately. He mentions Dionysius of Alexandria as having occupied the see in his own time; and Dionysius was bishop of Alexandria from AD 247 or 248 to AD 265. So also he speaks of Paul of Samosata as a contemporary; and Paul was deposed from his episcopate in AD 270. In the same way, having occasion to mention the great heresiarch of the age, he calls him "the maniac of yesterday and of our own times," while he himself elsewhere places Manes during the papacy of Felix (AD 270–274). And, speaking more generally, he draws the line between his own and a previous generation after his account of Dionysius of Alexandria, and before his mention of the accession of Dionysius of Rome (AD 259) and the troubles about Paul of Samosata which followed thereupon, declaring at this point that he intends now to relate the history of his own generation for the information of posterity. These notices will hardly allow us to place his birth much later than AD 260, so that he would be close upon eighty years old at the time of his death.

Nor again is any direct notice of his birthplace preserved in any early and trustworthy writer. It seems however tolerably safe to assume that he was a native of Palestine and probably of Cæsarea. We cannot indeed lay much stress on the fact that he is commonly called "Eusebius the Palestinian" for some designation was necessary to distinguish him from his namesake of Nicomedia, and

"Eusebius the Palestinian" is merely another way of saying "Eusebius of Cæsarea," which occurs in the same contexts. It may therefore refer to his see, rather than to his birthplace. But all the notices of his early life are connected with Cæsarea; and as it was usual in those times to appoint by preference to a bishopric some native of the place, everything is in favor of this as the city of his birth. The first writer who distinctly calls him a native of Palestine appears to be Theodorus Metochita, who flourished in the earlier part of the 14th century.

Of his parentage and relationships absolutely nothing is known. Nicephorus Callistus makes him a nephew of his friend, the martyr Pamphilus. Yet it is somewhat strange that he himself should never allude to this connexion, if it were so close. On the contrary, he speaks of his becoming acquainted with Pamphilus in such a manner as to suggest that there was no existing relationship which brought them together.

Whether he was a native of Cæsarea or not, it was with this city, the early home of Gentile Christianity, that all the associations of his youth, so far as we know, were connected. Here, as a child, he was catechized in that declaration of belief which years afterwards was laid by him before the great Council of Nicaea, and adopted by the assembled fathers as a basis for the creed of the universal Church. Here, as a young man, he remembered to have seen (AD 296) in company with the reigning Augustus, then on his progress through Palestine, a tall and handsome prince named Constantine. Here he listened to the Biblical expositions of the learned Dorotheus, thoroughly versed in the Hebrew Scriptures and not unacquainted with Greek literature and philosophy, once the superintendent of the emperor's purple factory at Tyre, but now a presbyter in the church of Cæsarea. Here, in due time, he was himself ordained a presbyter, probably by that bishop Agapius whose wise forethought and untiring assiduity and open-handed benevolence he himself has recorded. Here, above all, he contracted with the saintly student Pamphilus that friendship which was the crown and glory of his life, and which martyrdom itself could not sever.

Pamphilus, a native of Phœnicia, had studied in Alexandria, but was now settled in Cæsarea, of which church he was a presbyter. He had gathered about him a collection of books which seem to have been unrivalled in Christian circles, and which, supplemented by the excellent library of bishop Alexander at Jerusalem, enabled Eusebius to indulge to the full his portentous appetite for learning. Eusebius himself left a catalogue of the books contained in the library of Pamphilus. Jerome describes Pamphilus as gathering books together from all parts of the world, thus rivalling, in the domain of sacred learning, the zeal which Demetrius Phalercus or Pisistratus had shown for profane knowledge. Origen himself had set the example of a literary society. Aided by the munificence of his friend Ambrosius, he had kept about him always a large number of shorthand writers, to whom he dictated, and of calligraphers—women as well as men—who copied out the Scriptures for him. His example was not thrown away on Pamphilus.

Nor was it only in copying and editing that the society gathered about Pamphilus occupied itself. The work of translation would necessarily engage attention in a city which stood on the border land between the Greek and Syrian language. Amidst these and kindred pursuits the friendship between Pamphilus and Eusebius ripened. But Eusebius owed far more to Pamphilus than the impulse and direction given to his studies. Pamphilus was no mere student recluse. He was a man of large heart and bountiful hand. He was above all things helpful to his friends. He gave freely to all who were in want. He multiplied copies of the Scriptures, which he distributed gratuitously. And to the sympathy of the friend he united the courage of the hero. He had also the power of impressing his own strong convictions on others. Hence, when the great trial of faith came, his house was found to be not only the home of students but the nursery of martyrs.

To one like Eusebius, who owed his strength and his weakness alike to a ready susceptibility of impression from those about him, such a friendship was an inestimable blessing. How else could he express the strength of his devotion to this friend, who was more than a friend, than by adopting his name? He would henceforward be known as "Eusebius of Pamphilus." "In the midst of all," this glorious company of martyrs, writes Eusebius, "shone forth the excellency of my lord Pamphilus; for it is not meet that I should mention the name of that holy and blessed Pamphilus without styling him 'my lord'."

Eusebius was now in middle life when the last and fiercest persecution broke out. For nearly half a century—a longer period than at any other time since its foundation—the Church had enjoyed uninterrupted peace, so far as regards attacks from without. Suddenly and unexpectedly all was changed. The city of Cæsarea became a chief center of persecution. Eusebius tells us how he saw with his own eyes the houses of prayer razed to the ground, the holy Scriptures committed to the flames in the midst of the marketplaces, the pastors of the churches hiding themselves as they were hunted here and there, and shamefully jeered at when they were caught by their persecutors.

For seven years the attacks continued. They were fitful and intermittent. But the suspense and uncertainty must have increased the horror. No governor stayed his hands; no year was without its sufferers. Almost at any moment a devout and zealous Christian might be required to do that which his faith forbade him to do even at the cost of his life. Of some of the terrible scenes which ensued, Eusebius was himself an eyewitness. Of all he had the full and exact knowledge which is derived from immediate local and personal contact with the incidents. His written account shows how deeply he was impressed with the constancy and the triumphs of the sufferers. He tells of martyrs such as Procopius from Scythopolis, Alphaeus, the reader and exorcist in the church of Cæsarea, the blameless ascetic youth Apphianus, not yet twenty years of age, Ædesius, the brother of Apphianus, and many others, young and old, who endured and won the crown during this protracted reign of terror.

Above all others, Eusebius tells of that "name very dear to me," that " heavenly martyr of God," the "holy and blessed Pamphilus," who after two years of imprisonment sealed his long confession by martyrdom and crowned a saintly life with an heroic death, the center of a brave company, among whom he shone, "as the sun among the stars." For at this same time, eleven others perished with him. It was a perfect number, twelve in all, a type of the prophets and apostles. This happened under the governor Firmilianus, AD 309. It was the last spectacle on a grand scale displayed before men and angels in this arena of Christian fortitude. Not long after, the chief persecutor proclaimed his "palinode" to the world, and the Church had peace again.

And meanwhile, how had Eusebius borne himself in this season of peril? A quarter of a century later, when he was sitting in judgment at the council of Tyre, a grave charge was brought against him, affecting his conduct at this crisis. Potammon, bishop of Heraclea, an Egyptian confessor, started up and addressed the president, "Art thou seated as judge, Eusebius; and does Athanasius, innocent though he is, await his sentence from thee? Nay, tell me then, wast thou not with me in prison during the persecution? And I lost an eye for the truth, but thou, as we see, hast received no injury in any part of thy body, neither hast thou suffered martyrdom, but remained alive with no mutilation. How wast thou released from prison, unless it be that thou didst promise to those who put upon us the pressure of persecution to do that which is unlawful, or didst actually do it?" Eusebius, we are told, in vexation rose and dismissed the court, saying, "If ye come hither and say such things against us, then do your accusers speak the truth. For if ye behave thus tyrannously here, much more do ye in your own country."

On the strength of this charge he is supposed to have escaped martyrdom by offering sacrifice, or at least by some unworthy concession. But what does the evidence amount to? It is the language of a strong partisan, bitterly hostile to him; and it is after all only a conjectural inference of his accuser. There is a dignity in the response of Eusebius which bespeaks rather the disdainful innocence that will not condescend to a reply, than the uneasy conscience which shrinks from investigation. Even Athanasius, when referring to this incident, can only say that Eusebius was "accused of sacrificing" by the confessors. He does not dare to affirm that he was guilty. He himself obviously knows nothing of any such crime. He never elsewhere calls Eusebius "the sacrificer" as he does Asterius. If Eusebius had been guilty, this accusation would have been flung at him again and again, surrounded as he was by angry controversialists, in an age when controversy was not too scrupulous in its personalities.

So far as we have information of his movements at this time, they do not betray any such cowardice. During the long incarceration of his friend, Eusebius must have spent a great part of his time with him. Moreover, while the persecution raged, so far from avoiding the scenes of danger, Eusebius is found again and again in the thickest of the conflict. Not at Cæsarea alone does he appear as an eye-witness of the sufferings of the martyrs. At Tyre also he was present when several Christians were torn to pieces by the wild beasts in the amphitheater. Leaving Palestine, he visited Egypt. In no country did the persecution rage more fiercely than in Egypt. Here, in the Thebaid, they perished, ten or twenty, even sixty or a hundred, at a time. Eusebius relates how he himself, when he was in these parts, witnessed numerous martyrdoms in a single day, some by beheading, others by fire; the executioners relieving each other by relays in their hideous work, and the victims eagerly pressing forward to be tortured, clamoring for the honor of martyrdom, and receiving their sentence with joy and laughter. This visit to Egypt was apparently after the imprisonment and martyrdom of Pamphilus, in the latest and fiercest days of the persecution. If Potammon's taunt had any foundation in fact, it was probably now that Eusebius was imprisoned for his faith. If so, we have the less difficulty in explaining his release, without any stain left on his integrity or his courage.

It cannot have been very long after the restoration of peace (AD 313) when Eusebius was elected by unanimous consent to the vacant see of Cæsarea. The last bishop of this church whom he himself mentions is Agapius; and there is no reason for doubting that Eusebius was his immediate successor. Among the earliest results of the peace was the erection of a magnificent basilica at Tyre under the direction of his friend Paulinus, the bishop. Eusebius was invited to deliver the inaugural address. This oration is a paean of thanksgiving over the restitution of the Church, of which the splendid building at Tyre was at once the first-fruit and the type. This incident must have taken place not later than AD 315. For more than a quarter of a century he presided over the church of Cæsarea, winning, it would seem, the respect and affection of all. One attempt was made to translate him to a more important sphere, but it was foiled, as we shall see, by his own refusal. He died bishop of Cæsarea.

When the Arian controversy broke out, the sympathies of Eusebius were enlisted at an early stage on the side of Arius. If his namesake, Eusebius of Nicomedia, may be trusted, he was especially zealous on behalf of the Arian doctrine at this time. But the testimony of a strong partisan, eagerly seeking to place his cause in the best light, may well be suspected; and the attitude of Eusebius of Cæsarea throughout suggests that he was influenced rather by personal associations and by the desire to secure liberal treatment for the heresiarch than by any real accordance with his views. But, whatever may have been his motives, he wrote to Alexander, bishop of Alexandria, remonstrating with him for deposing Arius, and urging that he had misrepresented the opinions of the latter. Arius himself claims "all the bishops in the East," mentioning by name Eusebius of Cæsarea with others, as on his side. Accordingly, when he was deposed by a synod convened at Alexandria by Alexander, Arius at once appealed to Eusebius and others to interpose. A meeting of Syrian bishops was convened, and decided in favor of his restoration. The decision however was worded cautiously. The synod thought that Arius should be allowed to gather his congregation about him as heretofore; but they added that he must render obedience to Alexander and entreat to be admitted to communion with him.

Such was the attitude of Eusebius towards the Arian controversy when the Council of Nicaea assembled (AD 325). In this council he took a leading part. His prominence on this occasion he cannot have owed to his bishopric which, though important, did not rank with "the apostolic thrones" of Christendom—Rome, Antioch, and Alexandria. But he was beyond question the most learned man and the most famous living writer in the Church at this time. This fact alone must have secured a hearing for him. Probably however his importance was due even more to his close relations with the great emperor, Constantine. How this intimacy first grew up we do not know, but at this time he enjoyed the entire confidence of his imperial master.

It does not appear that Eusebius had any personal interview with Constantine when as a young man he passed through Cæsarea in the retinue of Diocletian. The historian records the incident merely as a sightseer. The first direct communication on record is a letter from the emperor to Eusebius as metropolitan of Cæsarea after the restoration of peace, giving orders for the rebuilding of the churches; but this does not suppose any personal acquaintance. Constantine indeed addresses him on this occasion as his "dearly beloved brother," but nothing can be built upon the expression. At the Council of Nicaea however he stood high in the emperor's favor, as the prominent position at the emperor's right hand shows. And from that time forward there seems to have been no interruption to his cordial relations with his imperial friend.

As the testimony in Eusebius's *Life of Constantine* demonstrates, the emperor was wont to enter into familiar conversation with him, relating to him the most remarkable incidents in his career, such as the miraculous appearance of the cross in the skies, and the protection afforded by this same emblem in battle. He corresponded with him on various subjects. Besides official letters, such as that which has been already mentioned, Constantine wrote to compliment him on his declining the see of Antioch. On receiving from Eusebius his treatise on the Paschal festival dedicated to himself, he sent in reply a letter of acknowledgment, expressing his excessive admiration and urging his correspondent to write many more such discourses. On another occasion again he writes to him, asking him to see to the execution of fifty copies of the Scriptures for his new capital Constantinople, and supplying him with the means necessary for executing the order.

But he not only corresponded familiarly with the bishop of Cæsarea. It was a still greater mark of respect to listen with patience, and even with delight, to the lengthy and elaborate orations which Eusebius held from time to time in his presence. We may well suppose that, beyond his vast learning, the bishop of Cæsarea had other qualities which rendered his society attractive to the great emperor. Constantine himself praises his gentleness or moderation. Nor would the unfeigned admiration which Eusebius entertained for his imperial host fail to recommend him to the great man. On the other hand, the bishop praises the frankness and affability of the sovereign, which was condescending and unsuspicious to a fault, so that the unscrupulous preyed upon his confidence.

Nor was Constantine the only member of the imperial family with whom Eusebius had friendly relations. We find the empress Constantia, the sister of Constantine and wife of Licinius, writing to him on a matter of religious interest. To her Eusebius replies in a letter, of which a great part is still extant. In his reply we are especially struck with the frankness of expostulation, almost of rebuke, which he addresses to this high personage.

It was probably owing to his favor with the imperial court that Eusebius delivered the opening address to Constantine when he took his seat in the council-chamber at Nicaea. The council was held during the emperor's vicennalia—his last rival and bitterest foe, Licinius, had been defeated and slain not long before—and the orator's address naturally took the form of a paean of victory, a hymn of thanksgiving. The speech is unfortunately not preserved, but we may form some notion of its probable character from the extant oration which Eusebius delivered at the tricennalia of this same sovereign.

When the main subject for which the council had been assembled came under discussion, we find Eusebius again taking a prominent part. He himself has left us an account of his doings at this stage in a letter of explanation which he afterwards wrote to his own church of Cæsarea. He laid before the council the creed which was in use in the Cæsarean church, which had been handed down to him from the bishops who preceded him, which he himself had been taught at his baptism, and in which, first as a presbyter and then as a bishop, he had instructed others. A number of amendments to the creed were offered by the several bishops and even by the emperor himself. But the Nicene creed as thus revised and ratified by the council fathers is still substantially the Cæsarean creed.

The hopes which Eusebius and others had built upon the decisions of the Nicene council were soon dashed. The final peace of the Church seemed as far distant as ever. In three controversies with three distinguished antagonists, Eusebius took a more or less prominent part, and his reputation, whether justly or not, has suffered greatly in consequence.

Eustathius, bishop of Antioch, was a staunch advocate of the Nicene doctrine and a determined foe of the Arians. Against Eusebius of Cæsarea he had already taken up a position of antagonism. He had assailed the tenets of Origen, of whom Eusebius was an ardent champion. He had attacked Eusebius himself, charging him with faithlessness to the doctrines of Nicaea, and was accused in turn of

Sabellianism by Eusebius. To the historian Socrates, the doctrines of the two antagonists appeared to have so much in common that he was puzzled to concede how they managed to fall out. At all events, Eustathius of Antioch and Eusebius of Cæsarea were regarded as the two principals in the quarrel.

A conflict so serious could not he confined to a paper war, and more active steps were taken. A synod of bishops was assembled at Antioch, AD 330, to consider the charge of Sabellianism brought against Eustathius. These charges were endorsed at the council and Eustathius was deposed. The see of Antioch thus became vacant and the assembled bishops put forward Eusebius of Cæsarea as his successor and wrote to the emperor on his behalf. It is not probable that such a position would at any time have possessed great attractions for Eusebius, and under the present circumstances it would appear less desirable than ever. He was a man of peace, and here was a prospect of war to the death. He was devoted to literary pursuits, and here it was proposed to tear him away from his Cæsarean library and from the comparative leisure of a less important see to the arduous duties of chief pastor in the most turbulent of cities. The splendors of a great patriarchate would hardly excite the ambition of such a man under these circumstances.

At all events, with the letter of the bishops pressing the appointment of Eusebius, the emperor received another from Eusebius himself declining the proffered honor. He alleged more especially the rule of the Church, which was regarded as an "apostolic tradition," forbidding translations from one see to another. In consequence of these representations, Constantine wrote three letters in reply which are preserved by Eusebius in his *Life of Constantine*. To the people of Antioch he sent a missive enforcing counsels of peace and deprecating their wish to rob another see of its bishop. To

Eusebius himself he wrote, highly applauding his decision and complimenting him in the highest terms. To the bishops he issued his injunctions that they should not seek to violate the apostolic rule, but that other fit persons should be put forward for election, of whom he mentioned two by name. One of these, Euphronius, was elected. Thus Eusebius remained undisturbed in the see of Cæsarea, which he retained till his death.

The next stage of the Arian controversy exhibits Eusebius in conflict with a greater personage than Eustathius. The disgraceful intrigues of the Arians and Meletians against Athanasius, which led to his first exile, are related in the biography of that saint. It is sufficient to say here that the emperor summoned Athanasius to appear before a gathering of bishops at Cæsarea, to meet the charges brought against him. It is stated by Theodoret that Constantine was induced to name Cæsarea by the counsels of the Arian party, who selected this place because the enemies of the accused were in a majority there. It is equally probable that the emperor would himself have given the preference to Cæsarea, since he reposed the greatest confidence in the moderation of its bishop. However this may be, Athanasius excused himself from attending. He believed, and he may have so pleaded in reply to the emperor, that there was a conspiracy against him, and that he would not have fair play at such a place. This was AD 334.

The matter however was not allowed to rest here. In the following year (AD 335), Athanasius received a peremptory and angry summons from Constantine to appear before a synod of bishops, not now at Cæsarea, but at Tyre. Theodoret conjectures that the place of meeting was changed by the emperor out of deference to the fears of Athanasius. The scenes at the synod of Tyre form the most picturesque and the most shameful chapter in the Arian controversy. After all allowance made for the exaggerations of the Athanasian party, from whom our knowledge is chiefly derived, the proceedings will still remain an undying shame to Eusebius of Nicomedia and his fellow intriguers. But there is no reason for supposing that Eusebius of Cæsarea took any active part in these plots.

The bishops assembled at Tyre were in the midst of their session, possibly preparing to crown the work of condemning and deposing Athanasius by the readmission of Arius and his friends into the church, when an urgent summons from the emperor, through the notary Marianus, called them to take part in the approaching festival at Jerusalem—the tricennalia of Constantine. No previous sovereign after Augustus, the founder of the empire, had reigned for thirty years. Constantine had a fondness for magnificent ceremonial, and here was a noble opportunity. The occasion was marked by the dedication of Constantine's new and splendid basilica, built on the site of Calvary. Bishops were summoned from all parts, the imperial posts were put at their disposal, and nothing was left undone to give lustre to the festival.

The prelates assembled at Tyre formed only a fraction of the subsequent gathering at Jerusalem. The festival was graced by a series of orations from the principal persons present, some pronouncing panegyrics on the emperor, others describing the magnificence of the building, others discoursing on high topics of theology, others interpreting the hidden meaning of the Scriptures. In these rhetorical displays Eusebius bore a conspicuous part. It is probable that Eusebius found in this dedication-festival a far more congenial atmosphere than in the intrigues and bickerings of the synod at Tyre. At all events, he treats the assemblage at Tyre as a mere episode of the festival at Jerusalem. The emperor, he says, preparing for the celebration of this festival, was anxious to put an end to the quarrels which rent the Church.

Arius and Euzoius had presented a confession of faith to the emperor, seeking readmission to the church. The emperor himself was satisfied with the opinions expressed in this document, and persuaded himself that it was in harmony with the faith of Nicaea. He therefore despatched Arius and Euzoius to Jerusalem, at the same time requesting the synod to consider their confession of faith, and to restore them to communion. The request was not made in vain. The condemnation of Athanasius at Tyre was followed by the re-admission of Arius and his followers at Jerusalem. Of the bishops who were responsible for this act, some would be instigated mainly by hostility to Athanasius, desiring thus to complete his defeat; others, taking the emperor's view, would regard it as an act of pacification. How far either motive would prevail with Eusebius of Cæsarea, we can only conjecture; but the stress which he lays on Constantine's desire to secure the peace of the church, on this as on all other occasions, suggests that pacification would be a predominant idea in his own mind, though perhaps not unmixed with other influences.

However, the conduct of the emperor at this time was strangely fickle and inconsistent. He had no distinct theological convictions on the great doctrine at issue, and was therefore at the mercy of the last speaker. Athanasius fled to Constantinople to plead his case and Constantine, though he desired pacification, was not insensible to justice. The personal pleadings of Athanasius convinced him that justice had been outraged. The bishops assembled at the dedication festival had scarcely executed the request, or the command, of the emperor's first letter, when they received another written in a very different temper. It was addressed "to the bishops that had assembled at Tyre" and it described their proceedings as "tumultuous and stormy." It further contended that their judgment had been overclouded by a spirit of contentiousness to the perversion of the truth, and it ended by summoning them to present themselves without a moment's delay at Constantinople. The leaders of the Eusebian party alone obeyed; the rest slunk away to their respective homes.

Among those who repaired to the imperial city was Eusebius of Cæsarea who, aside from the business of the council, found more congenial employment during his sojourn at Constantinople. The celebration of the emperor's tricennalia had not yet ended, and the bishop of Cæsarea delivered a panegyric. With complacent vanity the orator records in his *Life of Constantine* the emperor's satisfaction with his performance. This sovereign so "dear to God listened attentively, and was like one in an ecstasy of delight." He expressed his approval afterwards at a banquet to the bishops who were his guests. Possibly the delivery of this oration may have been the chief motive which induced Eusebius to accompany the Arian bishops to the imperial city. It must have been during this same visit also, though on an earlier day, that he delivered before the emperor his discourse on the Church of the Holy Sepulcher, which had probably been spoken previously at the dedication itself. On this occasion too, Eusebius reports in his *Life*, the satisfaction of Constantine was not less marked. He stood the whole time, though on the orator's own confession the discourse was lengthy. He refused again and again to be seated. He listened intently throughout, and would not suffer the orator to break off when he desired to do so.

Within twelve months, or a little more, of the time when he had listened with rapt attention to the orations of the bishop of Cæsarea, the great emperor, who then had seemed so strong and vigorous, breathed his last (May 22, AD 337).

The orator himself soon followed his imperial master. The precise time when Eusebius ended his long and laborious life is not known, but he was no longer living in 341, for we find his successor Acacius representing Cæsarea in the synod held at Antioch that year. From the connection in which his death is mentioned by the historians, we may infer that it happened not later than the close of AD 339 or the beginning of AD 340.

His literary activity was unabated to the end. Four years at the most can have elapsed between his last visit to Constantinople and his death. He must have been fast approaching his eightieth year when the end came. Yet at this advanced age, and within this short period, he composed the *Panegyric*, the *Life of Constantine*, the treatise *Against Marcellus*, and the companion treatise *On the Theology of the Church*; while probably also he had in hand at the same time other unfinished works, such as the *Theophania*. There are no signs of failing mental vigor in these latest works. The two doctrinal treatises, which must certainly be assigned to the last four years of his life, are perhaps the most forcible and lucid of his writings. The *Panegyric* and the *Life of Constantine* are disfigured indeed by a too luxuriant rhetoric, but in vigor they do not fall behind any of his earlier works.

Of his death itself no record is left. He passed away silently, we may suppose, as an old man of regular habits and equable temperament might be expected to pass away. Acacius, his successor, had been his pupil. Though more decidedly Arian in his bias, he was a devoted admirer of his master. He wrote a life of Eusebius, and seems to have edited some of his works.

The literary output of Eusebius was truly prodigious and a great deal of it has survived to this day. Often criticized as one who traded accuracy for rhetorical flourish, Eusebius was nonetheless a writer of tremendous ambition. Histories, apologies, exegetical works, dogmatic works, orations, sermons, and letters all flowed from his pen. Of his works, the most important, familiar and accessible to a modern audience remains his *Ecclesiastical History*, which gathers together an invaluable collection of anecdotes dating from the very beginning of the Church to Eusebius's own day.

Ranking immediately behind this work, both in terms of chronology and continuing interest to modern historians, is his *Life of Constantine*. The date of this work is fixed within narrow limits. It was written after the death of the great emperor who is its subject (May 337), and after his three sons had been declared Augusti (September 337). On the other hand, the death of the author himself was not later than AD 340. The work is not named indeed by Jerome, but then he himself implies that his catalogue is far from complete. On the other hand, it is directly mentioned by Socrates and largely used by writers of the 5th century, and it bears manifest traces of Eusebius's pen.

Eusebius does not profess to give a complete or general biography of Constantine. He distinctly states that he intends to pass over his military exploits and his legislative enactments, and to confine himself to those incidents which pertain to the religious life. Though not professing to be a continuation of the *Ecclesiastical History*, it fulfills this function to some extent. In this relation it is mentioned by Socrates, to whom, as to other historians of the same events, it furnishes important materials for the period to which it relates. For the Council of Nicaea more especially, and for some portions of the Arian controversy, it is a primary source of information of the highest value.

As regards the emperor himself, it is notoriously one-sided. The advice of Fleury to believe "everything bad which is told by Eusebius, and everything good which is told by Zosimus, of Constantine," will not easily be forgotten. A biography of this emperor, which does not even hint at the dark tragedy of the imperial household, when son and nephew and wife were murdered in rapid succession, must necessarily give a false and distorted impression of his character, whatever palliating circumstances for this crime we may discover or imagine. The verdict of Socrates, the earliest writer who mentions this work, will not be disputed. The author, he says, "has devoted more thought to the praises of the emperor and to the grandiloquence of language befitting a panegyric, as if he were pronouncing an encomium, than to the accurate narrative of the events which took place." But with all this there is no ground for suspecting him of misrepresenting the facts. Suppression rather than invention is the fault of the work. He has given us no shadow in his portrait, and Constantine's character was marked with some very dark lines.

With this important qualification, his biography has the highest value. It is a vivid picture of certain aspects of a great personality, painted by one who was familiarly acquainted with him and had access to important documents. It may be fulsome, and nauseous in its fulsomeness, but flattery is a word quite out of place. Flattery cannot pierce the sealed grave, and the language which he uses of the reigning sovereigns does not overstep the bounds of the conventional homage expected in those ages from a loyal subject. It may even be set down to the credit of Eusebius that his praises of Constantine are much louder after his death, than they ever were during his lifetime. Nor shall we do justice to Eusebius, unless we bear in mind the extravagant praises which even heathen panegyrists lavished on the great Christian emperor before his face, as an indication of the spirit of the age. But after all excuses made, this indiscriminate praise of Constantine is a reproach from which we should gladly have held Eusebius free.

In this work, as in several of his other writings, Eusebius has had no scruple in repeating himself. Some chapters are taken from the *Ecclesiastical History*; others from the *Tricennial Oration*; others again from the *Theophania*; but by far the greatest part of the work is original. Its most valuable portions are the letters and speeches of Constantine, and the author's personal reminiscences of the emperor. The headings of the chapters occasionally contain information which is not in the chapters themselves. They must therefore have been added by some one acquainted with the facts, and presumably a contemporary. If the reasons given by Valois for denying their Eusebian authorship be held valid, we may naturally attribute them to his successor Acacius, who inherited his papers and may possibly have published the *Life of Constantine* as a posthumous work.

In reviewing the literary history of Eusebius, we are struck first of all with the range and extent of his labors. His extant works, voluminous as they are, must have formed somewhat less than half of his actual writings. And, if the permanent utility of an author's labors may be taken as a test of literary excellence, Eusebius will hold a very high place indeed. In short, no ancient ecclesiastical writer has laid posterity under heavier obligations.

But beyond his learning he deserves the highest credit for the intelligent selection of his subjects. No writer has ever shown a keener insight in the choice of themes which would have a permanent interest for future generations. He lived on the confines of two epochs, separated from each other by one of those broad lines of demarcation which occur only at intervals of many centuries. He saw the greatness of the crisis; he seized the opportunity; he, and he only, preserved the past in all its phases, in history, in doctrine, in criticism, even in topography, for the instruction of the future.

This is his real title to greatness. As an expositor of facts, or as an abstract thinker, or as a master of style, it would be absurd to compare him with the great names of classical antiquity. His gigantic learning was his master rather than his slave. He had great conceptions, which he was unable adequately to carry out. He had valuable detached thoughts, but he fails in continuity of argument. He was most laborious, and yet most desultory. He accumulated materials with great diligence; he was loose and perfunctory and uncritical in the use of them once accumulated.

One other point deserves notice. While his writings cover so large an area and are so various in character, he is before all things an apologist. And doubtless his directly apologetic writings were much more effective than at this distance of time we can realize. But his part as an apologist does not end with his apologetic works. Whatever subject he touches, his thoughts seem to pour instinctively into this same channel. If he takes up the subject of chronology, a main purpose is to show the superior antiquity of the Hebrew oracles to the wisdom of the Greeks. If he sets himself to write a history of the Church, he does so because he sees in the course of events a vindication of the Divine Word, in whom the faith of the Christian centers. If he selects a theme so purely mundane as the encomium of a sovereign, he soars aloft at once into the region of theology, for he sees in the subject of his panegyric an instrument used by a higher power for the fulfilment of a Divine economy. If he employs himself to a task so essentially technical as the division of the Gospels into sections, his underlying motive is the desire to supply materials for a harmony, and thus to vindicate the essential unity of the evangelical narratives against gainsayers.

This character as an apologist was due partly to the epoch in which he lived, and partly to his individual temper and circumstances. To the epoch in which he lived—for his lot was cast in the great crisis of transition—he stood, as it were, on the frontier line between two ages, with one foot in the Hellenism of the past and the other in the Christianity of the future; and by his very position he was constrained to view them face to face, and to discuss their mutual relations. He was equally learned in the wisdom of the Greeks and in the teaching of the Scriptures, and his breadth of sympathy and moderation of temper fitted him beyond most of his contemporaries for the task of tracing their conflicts and coincidences.

If we may judge from the silence of his contemporaries— and silence in this case is an important witness—Eusebius commanded general respect by his personal character. With the single exception of the taunt of Potammon, which has been considered already, not a word of accusation is levelled against him in an age when theological controversy was peculiarly reckless and acrimonious. It is difficult to draw with any confidence the portrait of one of whose private acts so little is known. But we seem to see that his character was marked by amiability and moderation. His relations to Pamphilus, more especially, showed a strongly affectionate disposition; and it is more than probable that he was drawn into those public acts from which his reputation has suffered most, by the demands, or what seemed to him to be the demands, of private friendship. His moderation is especially praised, as we have seen, by the emperor Constantine, and his speculative opinions, as well as his personal acts, bear out this commendation.

He was not only the most learned and prolific writer of his age, but he administered the affairs of an important diocese, and he took an active part in all the great questions which agitated the Church. Not Athanasius himself was a harder worker in the cause of Christ. From youth to advanced age he labored with unremitting vigor. The self-sacrifices of the man of letters, if he is true to his calling, are not less in extent than those of the man of action, though they may be different in kind.

The excessive admiration of Eusebius for Constantine will be felt to need some apology. Yet it is not difficult to understand how he was led to this exaggerated estimate. Constantine was unquestionably one of the very greatest of the great emperors of Rome. His commanding personality must have been irresistible, and the impression thence derived would be enhanced by his deference towards the leading Christian bishops. The external circumstances of his reign moreover seemed to stamp it with a peculiar grandeur. He had ruled longer than any other emperor since Augustus, the founder of the empire. He had carried out a change in the relations between the Church and the State incomparably greater than any which had preceded, or than any which would follow. Eusebius delighted to place these two great sovereigns in juxtaposition. During the one reign the Word had appeared in the flesh; during the other He had triumphed over the world. The one reign was the counterpart and complement of the other.

This biography of Eusebius is extracted from:

Smith, William and Henry Wace. 1880. *A Dictionary of Christian Biography, Literature, Sects and Doctrines.* Volume 2. Little, Brown and Company: Boston.

TABLE OF CONTENTS

THE LIFE OF CONSTANTINE, BOOK I

THE LIFE OF CONSTANTINE, BOOK II

THE LIFE OF CONSTANTINE, BOOK III

THE LIFE OF CONSTANTINE, BOOK IV

TABLE OF CONTENTS

THE LIFE
OF THE BLESSED EMPEROR
CONSTANTINE

BOOK I

CHAPTER I

PREFACE—OF THE DEATH OF CONSTANTINE.

Already have all mankind united in celebrating with joyous festivities the completion of the second and third decennial periods of this great Emperor's reign: already, on the occasion of the first of these periods, have we ourselves received him as a triumphant conqueror in the assembly of God's ministers, and greeted him with the due meed of praise. And still more recently we have woven, as it were, garlands of eulogistic words, wherewith we encircled his sacred head in his own palace on the thirtieth anniversary of his reign.

But now, while I much desire[1] to give utterance to some of the sentiments I have been accustomed to entertain, I stand perplexed and doubtful which way to turn, being wholly lost in wonder at the extraordinary spectacle before me. For to whatever quarter I direct my view, whether to the east, or to the west, or over the whole world, or toward heaven itself, I see the blessed emperor everywhere present.

On earth I behold his sons, like some new reflectors of his brightness, diffusing everywhere the luster of their father's character; and I see him still living and powerful, and governing the general interests of mankind more completely than ever before, being multiplied as it were by the succession of his children to the Imperial power. They had indeed previously shared the dignity of Cæsars; but now, being invested with their father's entire authority, and graced by his accomplishments, for the excellence of their piety they are proclaimed by the titles of Sovereign, Augustus, Worshipful, and Emperor.

CHAPTER II

THE PREFACE CONTINUED.

And I am indeed amazed when I consider that he who was but lately visible and present with us in his mortal body, is still, even after death, when the natural thought disclaims all superfluous distinctions as unsuitable, most, marvelously endowed with the same imperial dwellings, and honors, and praises as heretofore. But further, when I raise my thoughts even to the arch of heaven, and there contemplate his thrice blessed soul in communion with God Himself, freed from every mortal and earthly vesture, and shining in a refulgent robe of light; and when I perceive that it is no more connected with the fleeting periods and occupations of mortal life, but honored with an ever-blooming crown, and an immortality of endless and blessed existence; I stand as it were entranced and deprived of all power of utterance. And so, while I condemn my own weakness, and impose silence on myself, I resign the task of speaking his praises worthily to one who is better able, even to Him who alone has power (being the immortal God, the Word), to confirm the truth of His own sayings.

CHAPTER III

HOW GOD HONORS PIOUS PRINCES, BUT DESTROYS TYRANTS.

And whereas He has given assurance that those who glorify and honor Him will meet with an ample recompense at His hands, while those who set themselves against Him as enemies and adversaries will compass the ruin of their own souls; already has He established the truth of these His own declarations. He has shown that the lives of those tyrants who denied and opposed Him have had a fearful end, and at the same time has made it manifest that even the death of His servant, as well as his life, is worthy of admiration and praise, and justly claims the memorial, not merely of perishable, but of immortal records.

Mankind have indeed devised some consolation for the frail and precarious duration of human life, and have thought by the erection of monuments to secure immortal honors to the memory of their ancestors. Some have employed the vivid delineations and colors of painting;[2] some have carved statues from lifeless blocks of wood; while others, by engraving their inscriptions deep on tablets and monuments of wood and stone, have sought to keep the virtues of those whom they honored in perpetual remembrance. All these indeed are perishable, and consumed by the lapse of time, being representations of the corruptible body, and incapable of expressing the image of the immortal soul. And yet these seemed sufficient to those who had no well-grounded hope of happiness after the termination of this mortal life. But God, that God, I say, who is the Preserver of the universe, has treasured up with Himself, for those who love godliness, greater blessings than human thought has conceived. And, by giving the earnest and first-fruits of future rewards even

3

here, assures, in some sort, immortal hopes to mortal eyes. The ancient oracles of the prophets, delivered to us in the Scripture, declare this. The lives of pious men, who shone in old time with every virtue, attest the same. And our own days prove it to be true, wherein Constantine, who alone of all that ever wielded the Roman power was the friend of God the Sovereign of all, has appeared to all mankind so bright an example of a godly life.

CHAPTER IV

HOW GOD HONORED CONSTANTINE.

And God Himself, whom Constantine worshipped, has confirmed this truth by the clearest manifestations of His will, being present to aid him at the commencement, during the course, and at the end of his reign, and holding him up to the human race as an exemplary pattern of godliness. Accordingly He has distinguished him alone of all the sovereigns of whom we have ever heard (by the manifold blessings He has conferred on him), as at once a mighty luminary and most distinct and powerful herald of genuine piety.

CHAPTER V

HE REIGNED ABOVE THIRTY YEARS, AND LIVED ABOVE SIXTY.

With respect to the duration of his reign, God honored him with three complete periods of ten years, and rather more, and limited the whole term of his mortal life to twice this number of years. And being pleased to make him a representative of His own sovereign power, He displayed him as the conqueror of the whole race of tyrants, and the destroyer of those godless great ones[3] of the earth who had ventured with desperate audacity to raise their impious arms against Him, the supreme King of the universe. They appeared indeed but for a very little space, and were destroyed together: while the one and only true God, when He had enabled His servant, clad in heavenly panoply, to stand singly against many foes, and by his means had relieved mankind from the multitude of the ungodly, constituted him a teacher of His worship to all nations, to testify with a loud voice in the hearing of all, that he acknowledged the true God, and turned with abhorrence from the error of them that are no gods.

CHAPTER VI

HE WAS THE SERVANT OF GOD, AND THE CONQUEROR OF NATIONS.

Thus, like a faithful and good servant, did he act and testify, openly declaring and owning himself the obedient minister of the supreme King. And God forthwith rewarded him, by making him ruler and sovereign, and victorious to such a degree that he alone of all the emperors pursued a continual course of conquest, unsubdued and invincible, and holding imperial power greater than tradition records to have been possessed by any before. So dear was he to God, and so blessed; so pious and so fortunate in all that he undertook, that with the greatest facility he compelled the submission of more nations than any who had preceded him, and yet retained his power, undisturbed, to the very close of his life.

CHAPTER VII

HE IS COMPARED WITH CYRUS KING OF THE PERSIANS, AND WITH ALEXANDER OF MACEDON.

Ancient history describes Cyrus as by far the most illustrious of all the Persian kings. And yet if we regard the end of his days,[4] we find it but little corresponded with his past prosperity, since he met with an inglorious and dishonorable death at the hands of a woman.

Again, the Greeks celebrate Alexander the Macedonian as the conqueror of very many and diverse nations; yet we find that he was removed by an early death, before he had reached the full vigor of manhood, being carried off by the effects of revelry and drunkenness. His whole life embraced but the space of thirty-two years, and his reign extended to no more than a third part of that period. Unsparing as the thunderbolt, he pursued his career of slaughter, and reduced entire nations and cities with all their inhabitants to slavery. But when he had scarcely arrived at the maturity of life, and was lamenting the loss of youthful pleasures, death fell upon him with terrible stroke, and (lest he should make still further havoc of the human race) cut him off in a foreign and hostile land, leaving no children to inherit his fame, and without a home to call his own. His kingdom too was instantly dismembered, each of his officers at once tearing away and seizing on a portion for himself. And yet this man is extolled for such deeds as these![5]

CHAPTER VIII

HE CONQUERED NEARLY THE WHOLE WORLD.

But our emperor began his reign at the time of life at which the Macedonian died, and lived as long again, and trebled the length of that prince's reign. And when he had confirmed his soldiers in the mild and sober precepts of godliness, he carried his arms as far as the Britons, and the nations that dwell in the very bosom of the Western ocean. He subdued likewise all Scythia, though situated in the remotest North, and divided into numberless diverse and barbarous tribes. He even pushed his conquests to the Blemmyans and Ethiopians, on the very confines of the South; nor did he think the acquisition of the Eastern nations unworthy his care. In short, diffusing the effulgence of his holy light to the ends of the whole world, even to the most distant Indians and other nations dwelling within the compass of the inhabited earth, he received the submission of all the rulers, governors, and satraps of barbarous nations, who cheerfully welcomed and saluted him, sending embassies and presents, and setting the highest value on his acquaintance and friendship, insomuch that they honored him with pictures and statues in their respective countries, and Constantine alone of all emperors was acknowledged and celebrated by all. Notwithstanding, even among these distant nations, he proclaimed the name of his God in his royal edicts with all boldness.

CHAPTER IX

HE WAS THE SON OF A PIOUS EMPEROR, AND BEQUEATHED THE IMPERIAL POWER TO HIS OWN SONS.

Nor did he give this testimony in words merely, while exhibiting failure in his own practice, but pursued every path of virtue, and was rich in the varied fruits of godliness. He ensured the affection of his friends by magnificent proofs of liberality, and inasmuch as he governed on principles of humanity, he caused his rule to be but lightly felt and acceptable to all classes of his subjects. Until at last, after a long course of years, and when he was wearied by his divine labors, the God whom he honored crowned him with an immortal reward, and translated him from a transitory kingdom to that endless life which He has laid up in store for the souls of His saints, after He had raised him up three sons to succeed him in his power.

As then the imperial throne had descended to him from his father, so, by the law of nature, was it reserved for his children and their descendants, and perpetuated (like some paternal inheritance) to endless generations. And indeed God Himself, who distinguished this blessed prince with divine honors while yet present with us, and who has adorned his death with choice blessings from His own hand, should be the writer of his actions; since He has recorded his labors and their successful results on tablets of heavenly memorial.

CHAPTER X

OF THE NECESSITY FOR THIS HISTORY, AND ITS VALUE IN A MORAL POINT OF VIEW.

However, hard as it is to speak worthily of this blessed character, and though silence were the safer and less perilous course, nevertheless it is incumbent on me, if I would escape the charge of negligence and sloth, to trace as it were a verbal portraiture, by way of memorial of the pious prince, in imitation of the delineations of human art. For I should be ashamed of myself were I not to employ my best efforts (feeble though they be and of little value), in praise of one who honored God with such surpassing devotion. I think too that my work will be on other grounds both instructive and necessary, since it will contain a description of those royal and noble actions of which God, the universal Sovereign, is pleased to approve. For surely it would be disgraceful that the memory of Nero, and other wicked and impious tyrants far worse than he, should meet with diligent writers to embellish the relation of their worthless deeds with elegant language, and record them in voluminous histories, and that I should be silent, to whom God Himself has vouchsafed such an emperor as all history records not, and has permitted me to come into his presence, and enjoy his acquaintance and familiar intimacy.

CHAPTER XI

HIS PRESENT OBJECT IS TO RECORD ONLY THE PIOUS ACTIONS OF CONSTANTINE.

Wherefore, if it is the duty of any one, it certainly is mine, to make an ample proclamation of his virtues to all in whom the example of noble actions is capable of inspiring the love of God. For some, who have written the lives of worthless characters, and the history of actions but little tending to the improvement of morals, from private motives either of gratitude or enmity, and possibly in some cases with no better object than the display of their own learning, have given an undue importance to their description of actions intrinsically base, by a refinement and elegance of diction. And thus they have communicated to others, who by the Divine favor had been kept apart from evil, the knowledge of conduct not only vile in itself, but deserving rather to be silenced in darkness and oblivion. But the course of my narrative, however unequal to the greatness of the deeds it has to describe, will yet derive luster even from the bare relation of noble actions. And surely the record of conduct that has been pleasing to God will afford a far from unprofitable, indeed a most instructive occupation, to persons of well-ordered minds.

It is my intention, however, to pass over very many of the royal deeds of this thrice blessed prince; as, for example, his conflicts and engagements in the field, his personal valor, his victories and successes against the enemy, and the many triumphs he obtained: likewise his provisions for the interests of individuals, his legislative enactments for the social advantage of his subjects, and a multitude of other imperial labors which are fresh in the memory of all. The design of my present undertaking leads me to speak and write of those circumstances only which have reference to his religious character. And, since these are themselves of almost infinite variety, I shall select from the facts which have come to my knowledge such as are most suitable, and worthy of lasting record, and endeavor to narrate them as briefly as possible. Henceforward indeed there is a full and free opportunity for celebrating in every way the praises of this most blessed prince, which hitherto we have been unable to do, on the ground that we are forbidden to judge any one blessed before his death,[6] because of the uncertain vicissitudes of life. Let me implore then the help of God, and may the inspiring aid of the heavenly Word be with me, while I commence my history from the very earliest period of his life.

CHAPTER XII

LIKE MOSES, HE WAS REARED IN THE PALACES OF ROYALTY.

Ancient history relates that a cruel race of tyrants oppressed the Hebrew nation; and that God, who graciously regarded them in their affliction, provided that the prophet Moses, who was then an infant, should be brought up in the very palaces and bosoms of the oppressors, and instructed in all the wisdom they possessed. And when he had arrived at the age of manhood, and the time was come for Divine justice to avenge the wrongs of the afflicted people, then the prophet of God, in obedience to the will of a more powerful Lord, forsook the royal household, and, estranging himself in word and deed from those by whom he had been brought up, openly preferred the society of his true brethren and kinsfolk. And in due time God exalted him to be the leader of the whole nation; and, after delivering the Hebrews from the bondage of their enemies, inflicted Divine vengeance through his means on the tyrant race. This ancient story, though regarded by too many as fabulous, has reached the ears of all. But now the same God has given to us to be eye-witnesses of miracles more wonderful than fables, and, from their recent appearance, more authentic than any report. For the tyrants of our day have ventured to war against the Supreme God, and have sorely afflicted His Church. And in the midst of these, Constantine, who was shortly to become their destroyer, but at that time of tender age, and blooming with the down of early youth, dwelt, as God's servant Moses had done, in the very home of the tyrants. Young, however, as he was, he shared not in the pursuits of the impious: for from that early period his noble nature (under the leading of the Divine Spirit), inclined him to a life of piety and acceptable service to God. A desire moreover to emulate the example of his father had its influence in stimulating the son to a virtuous course of conduct. The name of his father was Constantius (and we ought to revive his memory at this time), the most illustrious emperor of our age; of whose life it is necessary briefly to relate a few particulars, which tell to the honor of his son.

CHAPTER XIII

OF CONSTANTIUS HIS FATHER, WHO REFUSED TO IMITATE DIOCLETIAN, MAXIMIAN, AND MAXENTIUS, IN THEIR PERSECUTION OF THE CHRISTIANS.

At a time when four princes[7] shared the administration of the Roman empire, Constantius alone adopted a course of conduct different from that pursued by his colleagues, and avowed himself the friend of the Supreme God.

For while they besieged and wasted the churches of God, levelling them to the ground, and obliterating the very foundations of the houses of prayer, he kept his hands pure from their abominable impiety, and never in any respect resembled them.[8] They polluted their provinces by the indiscriminate slaughter of holy men and women; but he preserved himself free from the stain of this fearful crime: they, involved in the mazes of impious idolatry, enthralled first themselves, and then all under their authority, in bondage to the errors of evil demons; while he at the same time originated the profoundest peace throughout his dominions, and secured to his subjects the privilege of celebrating without hindrance the worship of God in short, while his colleagues oppressed all men by the most grievous exactions, and rendered their lives intolerable, and even worse than death, Constantius alone governed his people with a mild and tranquil sway, and exhibited towards them a truly parental and fostering care.[9]

Numberless indeed are the excellences of his character, which are the theme of praise to all; of these I will record one or two instances, as specimens of the quality of those which I must pass by in silence, and then I will proceed to the proposed course of my narrative.

CHAPTER XIV

HOW CONSTANTIUS HIS FATHER, BEING REPROACHED WITH POVERTY BY DIOCLETIAN, FILLED HIS TREASURY, AND AFTERWARDS RESTORED THE MONEY TO THOSE BY WHOM IT HAD BEEN CONTRIBUTED.

In consequence of the many reports in circulation respecting this prince, describing his kindness and gentleness of character, and the extraordinary elevation of his piety, alleging too, that by reason of his extreme indulgence to his subjects, he had not even a supply of money laid up in his treasury; the emperor who at that time occupied the place of supreme power sent to reprehend his neglect of the public weal, at the same time reproaching him with poverty, and alleging in proof of the charge the empty state of his treasury. On this he desired the messengers of the emperor to remain with him awhile, and, calling together the wealthiest of his subjects of all nations under his dominion, he informed them that he was in want of money, and that this was the time for them all to give a voluntary proof of their affection for their prince.

As soon as they heard this (as though they had long been desirous of an opportunity for showing the sincerity of their good will), with zealous alacrity they filled the treasury with gold and silver and other wealth, each eager to surpass the rest in the amount of his contribution: and this they did with cheerful and joyous countenances. And now Constantius desired the messengers of the supreme emperor personally to inspect his treasures, and directed them to give a faithful report of what they had seen; adding, that on the present occasion he had taken this money into his own hands, but that it had long been kept for his use in the custody of the owners, as securely as if under the charge of faithful treasurers. The ambassadors were overwhelmed with astonishment at what they had witnessed, and on their departure it is said that the truly generous prince sent for the owners of the property, and, after commending them severally for their obedience and true loyalty, restored it all, and bade them return to their homes.

This one circumstance, then, conveys a proof of the generosity of him whose character we are attempting to illustrate: another will bear the clearest testimony to his piety.

CHAPTER XV

OF THE PERSECUTION RAISED BY HIS COLLEAGUES.

By command of the supreme authorities of the empire, the governors of the several provinces had set on foot a general persecution of those who professed the worship of God. Indeed, it was from the imperial courts themselves that the very first of the pious martyrs proceeded, who passed through those conflicts which were the test of their faith, and most readily endured both fire and sword, and the depths of the sea—in short, every form of death—so that in a short time all the royal palaces were bereft of godly men. The result was that the authors of this wickedness were entirely deprived of the protecting care of God, since by their persecution of His worshippers they at the same time silenced the prayers that were wont to be made on their own behalf.

CHAPTER XVI

HOW CONSTANTIUS, FEIGNING IDOLATRY, EXPELLED THOSE WHO CONSENTED TO OFFER SACRIFICE, BUT RETAINED IN HIS PALACE ALL WHO WERE WILLING TO CONFESS CHRIST.

On the other hand, Constantius conceived an expedient full of sagacity, and carried it into effect, strange as it seems even to mention, but most of all remarkable in its execution.

He made a proposal to all the officers of his court, including even those in the highest stations of authority, offering them the following alternative: either that they should offer sacrifice to demons, and thus be permitted to remain with him, and enjoy their usual honors; or, in case

14

of refusal, that they should be shut out from all access to his person, and entirely disqualified from acquaintance and association with him. Accordingly, when they had individually made their selection, and the choice of each had been ascertained, then this admirable prince disclosed the secret meaning of his expedient, and condemned the cowardice and selfishness of the one party, while he highly commended the other for their conscientious devotion to God. He declared too, that those who had been false to their God must be unworthy of the confidence of their prince; for how was it possible that they should preserve their fidelity to him, who had proved themselves faithless to a higher power? He determined, therefore, that such persons should be removed altogether from the imperial court.

On the other hand, he intrusted with the guardianship of his person and empire those men whom the evidence of truth had proved to be worthy servants of God, declaring that they would manifest the same fidelity to their king, and that he was bound to treat such persons with special regard as his nearest and most valued friends, and to esteem them far more highly than the richest treasures.

CHAPTER XVII

OF HIS DEVOTION AND LOVE TO CHRIST.

The father of Constantine, then, is said to have possessed such a character as we have briefly described. And what, kind of death was vouchsafed to him in consequence of such devotion to God, and how far He whom he honored made his lot to differ from that of his colleagues in the empire, may be known to any one who will give his attention to the circumstances of the case. For after he had for a long time given many proofs of royal nobility of soul, in acknowledging the Supreme God alone, and condemning the polytheism of the impious, and had fortified his household by the prayers of holy men, he is said to have passed the remainder of his life in repose and tranquility, in the enjoyment of that happiness which consists in neither molesting others nor being molested ourselves.

Accordingly, during the whole course of his quiet and peaceful reign, he dedicated his entire household, his children, his wife, and domestic attendants, to the One Supreme God, so that the company assembled within the walls of his palace differed in no respect from a Church of God, wherein were also to be found His ministers, who offered continual supplications on behalf of their prince, and this at a time when, generally speaking, it was not allowable to make any allusion, even by name, to the worshippers of God.

CHAPTER XVIII

AFTER THE ABDICATION OF DIOCLETIAN AND MAXIMIAN, CONSTANTIUS BECAME CHIEF AUGUSTUS, AND WAS BLESSED WITH NUMEROUS OFFSPRING.

The immediate consequence of this conduct was a recompense from the hand of God, insomuch that he came into the supreme authority of the empire. For those princes who were his superiors in respect of age, for some unknown reason, resigned their power; and this sudden change took place in the first year which followed their persecution of the churches.

From that time Constantius alone received the honors of chief Augustus, having been previously indeed distinguished by the diadem of the imperial Cæsars, among whom he held the first rank; but after his worth had been proved in this capacity, he was invested with the highest dignity of the Roman empire, being named chief Augustus of the four who were afterwards elected to that honor. Moreover he surpassed most of the emperors in regard to the number of his family, having gathered around him a very large circle of male and female children. And, lastly, when he had attained to a happy old age, and was about to pay the common debt of nature, and exchange this life for another, God once more manifested His power in a special manner on his behalf, by providing that his eldest son Constantine should be present during his last moments, and ready to receive the imperial power from his hands.

CHAPTER XIX

OF HIS SON CONSTANTINE, WHO IN HIS YOUTH ACCOMPANIED DIOCLETIAN INTO PALESTINE.

For Constantine had been already accustomed to the society of his father's imperial colleagues, and had passed his time among them (like God's ancient prophet Moses), as we have said. And even in the very earliest period of his youth he was judged by them to be worthy of the highest honor. An instance of this we have ourselves seen, when he passed through Palestine with the senior emperor, at whose right hand he stood, and commanded the admiration of all who beheld him by the indications he gave even then of royal greatness. For no one was comparable to him for grace and beauty of person, or height of stature, and he so far surpassed his compeers in personal strength as to be a terror to them. He was, however, even more conspicuous for the excellence of his mental qualities than for his superior personal endowments, being gifted in the first place with a sound and temperate judgment, and having also reaped the advantages of a liberal education. He was also distinguished in no ordinary degree both by natural intelligence and divinely imparted wisdom.

17

CHAPTER XX

CONSTANTINE RETURNS TO HIS FATHER, IN CONSEQUENCE OF THE TREACHEROUS INTENTIONS OF DIOCLETIAN.

A youth thus proudly conspicuous soon attracted the notice of the emperors then in power, who observed his manly and vigorous figure and superior mind with feelings of jealousy and fear, and thence-forward carefully watched for an opportunity of inflicting some brand of disgrace on his character. But he, being aware of their designs (the details of which, through the providence of God, were more than once laid open to his view), sought safety in flight, and in this respect his conduct still affords a parallel to that of the great prophet Moses. Indeed, in every sense God was his helper, and He had before ordained that he should be present in readiness to succeed his father.

CHAPTER XXI

DEATH OF CONSTANTIUS, WHO LEAVES HIS SON CONSTANTINE EMPEROR.

Immediately therefore on his escape from the plots which had been thus insidiously laid for him, he made his way with all haste to his father, and arrived at length at the very time that he was lying at the point of death.[10] As soon as Constantius saw his son thus unexpectedly in his presence, he leaped from his couch, embraced him tenderly, and, declaring that the only anxiety which had troubled him in the prospect of death, namely that caused by the absence of his son, was now removed, he rendered thanks to God, and said that he now thought death better than the longest life. He next completed the arrangement of his private affairs, and took a final leave of the circle of sons and daughters by whom he was surrounded. And then, in his own palace, and on the imperial couch, he committed the administration of the empire, according to the law of nature, to his eldest son, and breathed his last.

CHAPTER XXII

AFTER THE BURIAL OF CONSTANTIUS, CONSTANTINE IS PROCLAIMED AUGUSTUS BY THE ARMY.

Nor did the imperial throne remain long unoccupied: for Constantine invested himself with his father's purple, and proceeded from the palace, presenting to all a renewal, as it were, in his own person, of his father's life and reign. He then conducted the funeral procession in company with his father's friends, some preceding, others following the train, and performed the last offices for the pious deceased with an extraordinary degree of magnificence.

Meantime all united in honoring this thrice blessed prince with acclamations and praises, and while with one common feeling they regarded the rule of the son as the restoration of the departed parent to life, they hastened at once to hail their new sovereign by the titles of Imperial and Worshipful Augustus, with joyful shouts. Thus the memory of the deceased emperor received honor from the praises bestowed upon his son, while the latter was pronounced blessed in being the successor of such a father. All the nations also under his dominion were filled with inexpressible joy and gladness at not being even for a moment deprived of the benefits of imperial government.

In the instance of the emperor Constantius, God has made manifest to our generation what the end of those is who in their lives have honored and loved Him.

CHAPTER XXIII

A BRIEF NOTICE OF THE DESTRUCTION OF THE TYRANTS.

With respect to the other princes, who persecuted and wasted the churches of God, I have not thought it fit to give any distinct account of their downfall, nor to stain the memory of the good by mentioning them in connection with those of an opposite character. The knowledge of the facts themselves will of itself suffice for the wholesome admonition of those who have witnessed or heard of the evils which severally befell them.

CHAPTER XXIV

IT WAS BY THE WILL OF GOD THAT CONSTANTINE BECAME POSSESSED OF THE EMPIRE.

Thus then the God of all, the Supreme Governor of the world, by His own will appointed Constantine, the descendant of so renowned a parent, to be prince and sovereign: so that, while others have been raised to this distinction by the election of their fellow-men, he is the only one to whose elevation no mortal may boast of having contributed.

CHAPTER XXV

VICTORIES OF CONSTANTINE OVER THE BARBARIANS AND THE BRITONS.

As soon then as he was established on the throne, he began to care for the interests of his paternal inheritance, and visited with much considerate kindness all those provinces which had previously been under his father's government. Some tribes of the barbarians who dwelt on the banks of the Rhine, and the shores of the Western ocean, having ventured to revolt, he reduced them all to obedience, and brought them from their savage state to one of gentleness and submission. He contented himself with checking the inroads of others, and drove from his dominions, like untamed and savage beasts, those whom he perceived to be altogether incapable of the settled order of civilized life. Having disposed of these affairs to his satisfaction, he directed his attention to other quarters of the world, and first passed over to the British nations,[11] which lie in the very bosom of the ocean. These he reduced to submission, and then proceeded to consider the state of the remaining portions of the empire, that he might be ready to tender his aid wherever circumstances might require it.

CHAPTER XXVI

HE RESOLVES TO DELIVER ROME FROM THE TYRANNY OF MAXENTIUS.

While therefore he regarded the entire world as one immense body, and perceived that the head of it all, the royal city of the Roman empire, was bowed down by the weight of a tyrannous oppression, at first he had left the task of liberation to those who governed the other divisions of the empire, as being his superiors in point of age. But when none of these proved able to afford relief, and those who had attempted it had experienced a disastrous termination of their enterprise, he said that life was without enjoyment to him as long as he saw the imperial city thus afflicted, and prepared himself for the effectual suppression of the tyranny.[12]

CHAPTER XXVII

AFTER REFLECTING ON THE DOWNFALL OF THOSE WHO HAD WORSHIPPED IDOLS, HE MADE CHOICE OF CHRISTIANITY.

Being convinced, however, that he needed some more powerful aid than his military forces could afford him, on account of the wicked and magical enchantments which were so diligently practiced by the tyrant, he began to seek for Divine assistance, deeming the possession of arms and a numerous soldiery of secondary importance, but trusting that the cooperation of a Deity would be his security against defeat or misfortune. He considered, therefore, on what God he might rely for protection and assistance.

While engaged in this inquiry, the thought occurred to him, that, of the many emperors who had preceded him, those who had rested their hopes in a multitude of gods, and served them with sacrifices and offerings, had in the first place been deceived by flattering predictions, and oracles which promised them all prosperity, and at last had met with an unhappy end, while not one of their gods had stood by to warn them of the impending wrath of Heaven. On the other hand he recollected that his father, who had pursued an entirely opposite course, who had condemned their error, and honored the one Supreme God during his whole life, had found Him to be the Savior and Protector of his empire, and the Giver of every good thing. Reflecting on this, and well weighing the fact that they who had trusted in many gods had also fallen by manifold forms of death, without leaving behind them either family or offspring, stock, name, or memorial among men; and considering further that those who had already taken arms against the tyrant, and had marched to the battle field under the protection of a multitude of gods, had met with a

22

dishonorable end (for one of them had shamefully retreated from the contest without a blow, and the other, being slain in the midst of his own troops, had become as it were the mere sport of death); reviewing, I say, all these considerations, he judged it to be folly indeed to join in the idle worship of those who were no gods, and, after such convincing evidence, to wander from the truth; and therefore felt it incumbent on him to honor no other than the God of his father.

CHAPTER XXVIII

HOW, WHILE HE WAS PRAYING, GOD SENT HIM A VISION OF A CROSS OF LIGHT IN THE HEAVENS AT MID-DAY, WITH AN INSCRIPTION ADMONISHING HIM TO CONQUER BY THAT.

Accordingly he called on Him with earnest prayer and supplications that He would reveal to him who He was, and stretch forth His right hand to help him in his present difficulties. And while he was thus praying with fervent entreaty, a most marvelous sign appeared to him from heaven, the account of which it might have been difficult to receive with credit, had it been related by any other person. But since the victorious emperor himself long afterwards declared it to the writer of this history, when he was honored with his acquaintance and society, and confirmed his statement by an oath, who could hesitate to accredit the relation, especially since the testimony of after-time has established its truth? He said that about mid-day, when the sun was beginning to decline, he saw with his own eyes the trophy of a cross of light in the heavens, above the sun, and bearing the inscription, CONQUER BY THIS. At this sight he himself was struck with amazement, and his whole army also, which happened to be following him on some expedition, and witnessed the miracle.

CHAPTER XXIX

HOW THE CHRIST OF GOD APPEARED TO HIM IN HIS SLEEP, AND COMMANDED HIM TO USE IN HIS WARS A STANDARD MADE IN THE FORM OF A CROSS.[13]

He said, moreover, that he doubted within himself what the import of this apparition could be. And while he continued to ponder and reason on its meaning, night imperceptibly drew on; and in his sleep the Christ of God appeared to him with the same sign which he had seen in the heavens, and commanded him to procure a standard made in the likeness of that sign, and to use it as a safeguard in all engagements with his enemies.

CHAPTER XXX

THE MAKING OF THE STANDARD OF THE CROSS.

At dawn of day he arose, and communicated the secret to his friends: and then, calling together the workers in gold and precious stones, he sat in the midst of them, and described to them the figure of the sign he had seen, bidding them represent it in gold and precious stones. And this representation I myself have had an opportunity of seeing.

CHAPTER XXXI

A DESCRIPTION OF THE STANDARD OF THE CROSS, WHICH THE ROMANS NOW CALL THE LABARUM.[14]

Now it was made in the following manner. A long spear, overlaid with gold, formed the figure of the cross by means of a piece transversely laid over it. On the top of the whole was fixed a crown, formed by the intertexture of gold and precious stones; and on this, two letters indicating the name of Christ, symbolized the Savior's title by means of its first characters,[15] the letter P being intersected by X exactly in its center: and these letters the emperor was in the habit of wearing on his helmet at a later period. From the transverse piece which crossed the spear was suspended a kind of streamer of purple cloth, covered with a profuse embroidery of most brilliant precious stones; and which, being also richly interlaced with gold, presented an indescribable degree of beauty to the beholder. This banner was of a square form, and the upright staff, which in its full extent was of great length, bore a golden half-length portrait of the pious emperor and his children on its upper part, beneath the trophy of the cross, and immediately above the embroidered streamer.

The emperor constantly made use of this salutary sign as a safeguard against every adverse and hostile power, and commanded that others similar to it should be carried at the head of all his armies.

CHAPTER XXXII

CONSTANTINE RECEIVES INSTRUCTION, AND READS THE SACRED SCRIPTURES.

These things were done shortly afterwards. But at the time above specified, being struck with amazement at the extraordinary vision, and resolving to worship no other God save Him who had appeared to him, he sent for those who were acquainted with the mysteries of His doctrines, and inquired who that God was, and what was intended by the sign of the vision he had seen.

They affirmed that He was God, the only begotten Son of the one and only God: that the sign which had appeared was the symbol of immortality, and the trophy of that victory over death which He had gained in time past when sojourning on earth. They taught him also the causes of His advent, and explained to him the true account of His incarnation. Thus he sought instruction in these matters, but was still impressed with wonder at the divine manifestation which had been presented to his sight. Comparing, therefore, the heavenly vision with the interpretation given, he found his judgment confirmed; and, in the persuasion that the knowledge of these things had been imparted to him by Divine teaching, he determined thenceforth to devote himself to the perusal of the inspired writings.

Moreover, he made the priests of God his counselors, and deemed it incumbent on him to honor the God who had appeared to him with all devotion. And after this, being fortified by well-grounded hopes in Him, he undertook to quench the fury of the fire of tyranny.

CHAPTER XXXIII

OF THE ADULTEROUS CONDUCT OF MAXENTIUS AT ROME.

For he who had tyrannically possessed himself of the imperial city, had proceeded to great lengths in impiety and wickedness, so as to venture without hesitation on every vile and impure action. For example: he would part lawfully-married women from their husbands, and after most grievously dishonoring them, send them back to their husbands. And these insults he offered not to men of mean or obscure condition, but to those who held the first places in the Roman senate. Moreover, though he shamefully dishonored almost numberless free women, he was unable to satisfy his ungoverned and intemperate desires. But when he essayed to corrupt Christian women also, he could no longer secure success to his designs, since they chose rather to expose their lives to death than yield their persons to be defiled by him.

CHAPTER XXXIV

HOW THE WIFE OF A PREFECT SLEW HERSELF TO PRESERVE HER CHASTITY.

Now a certain woman, wife of one of the senators who held the authority of Prefect in the city, when she understood that those who ministered to the tyrant's lusts were standing before her house (she was a Christian), and knew that her husband through fear had bidden them take her and lead her away, begged a short space of time for arraying herself in her usual dress, and entered her chamber. There, being left alone, she sheathed a sword in her own breast, and immediately expired, leaving indeed her dead body to her conductors, but declaring to all mankind, both to present and future generations, by an act which spoke louder than any words, that the chastity for which Christians are famed is alone invincible and not to be destroyed. Such was the conduct displayed by this woman.

CHAPTER XXXV

MASSACRE OF THE ROMAN PEOPLE BY MAXENTIUS.

All men, therefore, both people and magistrates, whether of high or low degree, trembled through fear of him whose daring wickedness was such as I have described, and were oppressed by his grievous tyranny. Nay, though they submitted quietly, and endured this bitter servitude, still there was no escape from the tyrant's sanguinary cruelty. For at one time, on some trifling pretence, he exposed the populace to be slaughtered by his own body-guard; and countless multitudes of the Roman people were slain in the very midst of the city by the lances and weapons, not of Scythians or barbarians, but of their own fellow-citizens. And besides this, it is impossible to calculate the number of senators whose blood was shed with a view to the seizure of their respective estates, since at different times and on various fictitious charges, multitudes of them suffered death.

CHAPTER XXXVI

MAGIC ARTS OF MAXENTIUS AGAINST CONSTANTINE, AND FAMINE AT ROME.

But the crowning point of the tyrant's wickedness was his having recourse to sorcery—sometimes for magic purposes opening women with child, at other times searching into the bowels of new-born infants. He slew lions also, and practiced certain horrid arts for evoking demons, and averting the approaching war, hoping by these means to make himself secure of victory. In short, it is impossible to describe the manifold acts of oppression by which this tyrant of Rome enslaved his subjects, so that by this time they were reduced to the most extreme penury and want of necessary food, a scarcity such as our contemporaries do not remember ever before to have existed at Rome.

CHAPTER XXXVII

DEFEAT OF MAXENTIUS'S ARMIES IN ITALY.

Constantine, however, filled with compassion on account of all these miseries, began to arm himself with all warlike preparation against the tyranny. Assuming therefore the Supreme God as his patron, and invoking His Christ to be his preserver and aid, and setting the victorious trophy, the salutary symbol, in front of his soldiers and body-guard, he marched with his whole forces, eager to reinstate the Romans in the freedom they had inherited from their ancestors. And whereas, Maxentius, trusting more in his magic arts than in the affection of his subjects, dared not even advance outside the city gates, but had guarded every place and district and city subject to his tyranny, with large bodies of soldiers and numberless ambuscades. The emperor, confiding in the help of God, advanced against the first and second and third divisions of the tyrant's forces, defeated them all with ease at the first assault, and made his way into the very interior of Italy.

CHAPTER XXXVIII

DEATH OF MAXENTIUS ON THE BRIDGE OF THE TIBER.

And already he was approaching very near Rome itself when, to save him from the necessity of fighting with all the Romans for the tyrant's sake, God Himself drew the tyrant, as it were by secret cords, a long way outside the gates.

And now those miracles recorded in Holy Writ, which God of old wrought against the ungodly (discredited by most as fables, yet believed by the faithful), did He in very deed confirm to all alike, believers and unbelievers, who were eye-witnesses of the wonders I am about to relate. For as once in the days of Moses and the Hebrew nation, who were worshippers of God, cast Pharaoh's chariots and his host into the waves, and drowned his chosen chariot-captains in the Red Sea, so at this time did Maxentius, and the solders and guards with him, sink to the bottom as a stone, when, in his flight before the divinely-aided forces of Constantine, he essayed to cross the river which lay in his way, over which he had made a strong bridge of boats, and had framed an engine of destruction, really against himself, but in the hope of ensnaring thereby him who was beloved by God. For his God stood by the one to protect him, while the other, destitute of His aid, proved to be the miserable contriver of these secret devices to his own ruin. So that one might well say, "He made a pit, and digged it, and shall fall into the ditch which he made. His mischief shall return upon his own head, and his iniquity shall come down upon his own pate."[16] Thus, in the present instance, under divine direction, the machine erected on the bridge, with the ambuscade concealed therein, giving way unexpectedly before the appointed time, the passage began to sink down, and the boats with the men in them went bodily to the bottom. And first the wretch himself, then his armed attendants and guards, even as the sacred oracles had before described, "sank as lead in the mighty waters."[17] So that they who thus obtained victory from God might well, if not in the same words, yet in fact in the same spirit as the people of His great servant Moses, sing and speak as they did concerning the impious tyrant of old: "Let us sing unto the Lord, for He has been glorified exceedingly: the horse and his rider has He thrown into the sea. He is become my helper and my shield unto salvation." And again, "Who is like to Thee, O Lord, among the gods? Who is like Thee, glorious in holiness, marvellous in praises, doing wonders?"[18]

CHAPTER XXXIX

CONSTANTINE'S ENTRY INTO ROME.

Having then at this time sung these and such-like praises to God, the Ruler of all and the Author of victory, after the example of His great servant Moses, Constantine entered the imperial city in triumph. And here the whole body of

30

the senate, and others of rank and distinction in the city, freed as it were from the restraint of a prison, along with the whole Roman populace, their countenances expressive of the gladness of their hearts, received him with acclamations and excess of joy; men, women and children, with countless multitudes of servants, greeting him as deliverer, preserver, and benefactor, with incessant shouts. But he, being possessed of inward piety toward God, was neither rendered arrogant by these plaudits, nor uplifted by the praises he heard: but, being sensible that he had received help from God, he immediately rendered a thanksgiving to Him as the Author of his victory.

CHAPTER XL

OF THE STATUE OF CONSTANTINE HOLDING A CROSS, AND ITS INSCRIPTION.

Moreover by many[19] writings and monumental inscriptions he made known to all men the salutary symbol, setting up this great trophy of victory over his enemies in the midst of the imperial city, and expressly causing it to be engraven in indelible characters, that the salutary sign was the preservative of the Roman government and of the entire empire. Accordingly, he immediately ordered a lofty spear in the figure of a cross to be placed beneath the hand of a statue representing himself, in the most frequented part of Rome, and the following inscription to be engraved on it, in the Latin language:—BY VIRTUE OF THIS SALUTARY SIGN, WHICH IS THE TRUE SYMBOL OF VALOR, I HAVE PRESERVED AND LIBERATED YOUR CITY FROM THE YOKE OF TYRANNY. I HAVE ALSO SET AT LIBERTY THE ROMAN SENATE AND PEOPLE, AND RESTORED THEM TO THEIR ANCIENT GREATNESS AND SPLENDOR.

CHAPTER XLI

REJOICINGS THROUGHOUT THE PROVINCES; AND CONSTANTINE'S ACTS OF GRACE.

Thus the pious emperor, glorying in the confession of the victorious cross, proclaimed the Son of God to the Romans with great boldness of testimony. And all the inhabitants of the city with one consent, both senate and people, reviving as it were from the pressure of a bitter and tyrannical domination, seemed to enjoy the rays of a purer light, and to experience the renovating power of a fresh and new existence. All the nations too, as far as the limit of the western ocean, being set free from the calamities which had heretofore distressed them, and gladdened by joyous festivals, ceased not to praise him as the victorious, the pious, the common benefactor. All indeed, with one voice and one mouth, declared that Constantine had appeared through the special favor of God as a general blessing to mankind. The imperial edict also was everywhere published, whereby those who had been wrongfully deprived of their estates were permitted again to enjoy their own, while those who had unjustly suffered exile were recalled to their homes. Moreover, he freed from imprisonment, and from every kind of danger and fear, those who by reason of the tyrant's cruelty had been subject to these sufferings.

CHAPTER XLII

OF THE HONORS CONFERRED UPON BISHOPS, AND THE BUILDING OF CHURCHES.

The emperor was also accustomed personally to invite the society of God's ministers, whom he distinguished with the highest possible respect and honor, treating them in every sense as persons consecrated to the service of his God. Accordingly, they were admitted to his table, though mean in their attire and outward appearance; yet not so in his estimation, since he judged not of their exterior as seen by the vulgar eye, but thought he discerned in them somewhat of the character of God Himself. He made them also his companions in travel, believing that He whose servants they were would thus be more favorably inclined to himself. Besides this, he gave from his own private resources costly benefactions to the Churches of God, both enlarging and heightening the sacred edifices, and embellishing the august sanctuaries of the Church with abundant offerings.

CHAPTER XLIII

CONSTANTINE'S LIBERALITY TO THE POOR.

He likewise distributed money largely to those who were in need. And not only so, but his kindness and beneficence extended even to the heathen who had no claim on him. And he provided not money only, or necessary food, but also decent clothing for the poor outcasts who begged alms in the forum. But in the case of those who had once been prosperous, and had experienced a reverse of circumstances, his aid was still more lavishly bestowed. On such persons, in a truly royal spirit, he conferred magnificent benefactions, giving grants of land to some, and honoring others with various offices of trust. To unfortunate orphans he sustained the relation of a careful father, while he relieved the forlorn condition of widows, and cherished them with special care. Nay, he even gave virgins, left unprotected by their parents' death, in marriage to wealthy men with whom he was personally acquainted. But this he did after first bestowing on the brides such portions as it was fitting they should bring to their future husbands. In short, as the sun, when he rises upon the earth, liberally imparts his rays of light to all, so did Constantine, proceeding at early dawn from the imperial palace, and rising as it were with the heavenly luminary, impart the rays of his own beneficence to all who approached his person. It was scarcely possible to be near him without receiving some benefit, nor did it ever happen that any who had expected to obtain his assistance were disappointed in their hope.

CHAPTER XLIV

HOW HE WAS PRESENT AT THE SYNODS OF BISHOPS.

Such, then, was his general conduct towards all. But he exercised a peculiar care over the Church of God. And whereas, in the several provinces there were some who differed from each other in judgment, he assumed as it were the functions of a general bishop constituted by God, and convened synods of His ministers. Nor did he disdain to be present and sit with them in their assembly, but bore a share in their deliberations, endeavoring to minister to them all what pertained to the peace of God. He took his seat too in the midst of them, as an individual amongst many, dismissing his guards and soldiers, and all whose duty it was to defend his person; feeling himself sufficiently protected by the fear of God, and secure in the affection of his most faithful Christian friends. Those whom he saw inclined to a sound judgment, and exhibiting a calm and conciliatory temper, received his high approbation, for he evidently delighted in a general harmony of sentiment; while he regarded the refractory and obstinate with aversion.

CHAPTER XLV

HOW HE BORE WITH IRRATIONAL OPPONENTS.

Moreover he endured with patience some who were exasperated against himself, directing them in mild and gentle terms to conduct themselves with temper, and not excite seditious tumults. And some of these respected his admonitions, and desisted. But as to those who proved incapable of sound judgment, he left them entirely at the disposal of God, and never himself resolved on severe measures against any one. Hence it naturally happened that the disaffected in Africa advanced so far in a course of licentiousness as even to venture on overt acts of audacity; some evil spirit, as it seems probable, being jealous of the present great prosperity, and impelling these men to atrocious deeds, that he might excite the emperor's anger against them. He gained nothing, however, by this malicious conduct; for the emperor treated these proceedings with contempt, and declared that he recognized their origin to be from the evil one, inasmuch as these were not the actions of sober persons, but of those who were either utterly devoid of reason, or else possessed by some evil spirit, and that such should be pitied rather than punished,[20] since, though justice might check the fury of mad-men, refined humanity had rather sympathize with their condition.

CHAPTER XLVI

VICTORIES OVER THE BARBARIANS.

Thus the emperor in all his actions honored God the Controller of all things, and exercised an unwearied oversight over His churches. And God requited him, by subduing all barbarous nations under his feet, so that he was able everywhere to raise trophies over his enemies. And He proclaimed his name as conqueror to all mankind, and made him a terror to his adversaries—not indeed that this was his natural character, since he was rather the meekest, and gentlest, and most benevolent of men.

CHAPTER XLVII

DEATH OF MAXIMIAN, WHO HAD ATTEMPTED A CONSPIRACY, AND OF OTHERS WHOM CONSTANTINE DETECTED BY DIVINE REVELATION.

While he was thus engaged, the second of those who had resigned the throne being detected in a treasonable conspiracy, suffered a most ignominious death.[21] He was the first whose pictures, statues, and all similar marks of honor and distinction were everywhere destroyed, on the ground of his crimes and impiety. After him others also of the same family were discovered in the act of framing secret machinations against the emperor; all their intentions being miraculously revealed by God through visions to His servant.

For He frequently vouchsafed to him manifestations of Himself, the Divine presence appearing to him in a most marvellous manner, and according to him manifold intimations of future events. Indeed it is impossible to describe in words the inexpressible wonders of divine grace which God was pleased to vouchsafe to His servant. Surrounded by these, he passed the residue of his life in security, rejoicing in the true affection of his subjects, rejoicing too because he saw all beneath his government leading contented and peaceful lives; but above all delighted at the flourishing condition of the churches of God.

CHAPTER XLVIII

CELEBRATION OF CONSTANTINE'S DECENNALIA.

While he was thus circumstanced, he completed the tenth year of his reign. On this occasion he ordered the celebration of general festivals, and offered thanksgivings to God the Supreme King, as pure sacrifices free from flame and smoke. And from this employment he derived much pleasure, not so from the tidings he received of the ravages committed in the Eastern provinces.

CHAPTER XLIX

IN WHAT MANNER LICINIUS OPPRESSED
THE EAST.

For he was informed that in that quarter a certain savage beast was besetting both the Church of God and the other inhabitants of the provinces, owing, as it were, to the efforts of the evil spirit to produce effects quite contrary to the deeds of the pious emperor—so that the Roman empire, divided into two parts, seemed to all men to resemble night and day, since darkness overspread the provinces of the East, while the brightest day illumined the inhabitants of the opposite portion. And whereas the latter were receiving manifold blessings at the hand of God, the sight of these blessings proved intolerable to that envy which hates all good, as well as to the tyrant who afflicted the other division of the empire, and who, notwithstanding that his government was prospering, and he had been honored by affinity with so great an emperor as Constantine, yet cared not to follow the steps of that pious prince, but strove rather to imitate the evil purposes and practice of impious men, choosing to adopt their counsels, of whose ignominious end he had himself been an eye-witness, rather than to maintain amicable relations with him who was his superior.

CHAPTER L

LICINIUS ATTEMPTS A CONSPIRACY AGAINST CONSTANTINE.

Accordingly he engaged in an irreconcilable war against his benefactor, altogether regardless of the laws of friendship, the obligation of oaths, the ties of kindred, and already existing treaties. For the most benignant emperor had given him a proof of sincere affection in bestowing on him the hand of his sister, thus granting him the privilege of a place in family relationship and his own ancient imperial descent, and investing him also with the rank and dignity of his colleague in the empire. But the other, in a spirit the very opposite to this, employed himself in machinations against his superior, and devised various means for ungratefully invading his benefactor's tranquillity. At first, under the specious mask of friendship, he conducted all his plots with art and treachery, expecting thus to succeed in concealing his designs. But God enabled His servant to detect the schemes thus darkly devised. Licinius, however, being discovered in his first attempts, had recourse to fresh frauds—at one time pretending friendship, at another claiming confidence on the ground of solemn treaties—then at once violating every engagement, and again beseeching pardon by embassies, yet after all foully falsifying his word: till at last he declared open war, and with desperate infatuation resolved thenceforward to carry arms against God Himself, whose worshipper he knew the emperor to be.

CHAPTER LI

TREACHEROUS ARTS OF LICINIUS AGAINST THE BISHOPS, AND HIS PROHIBITION OF SYNODS.

And at first he made secret inquiry respecting the ministers of God subject to his dominion (and who had never in any respect offended against his government), and with industrious malice sought occasions of accusation against them. And when he found himself at a loss to substantiate any charge, or find a real ground of objection against them, he next enacted a law, to the effect that the bishops should never on any account hold communication with each other, nor should any one of them be permitted to absent himself on a visit to a neighboring church; nor, lastly, should the holding of synods, or councils for the consideration of affairs of common interest, be further sanctioned. Now this was clearly a pretext for displaying his malice against us.[22] For we were compelled either to violate the law, and thus be amenable to punishment, or else, by compliance with its injunctions, to nullify the statutes of the Church inasmuch as it is impossible to bring important questions to a satisfactory adjustment, except by means of synods. In other cases also this enemy of God, being determined to act in opposition to our pious prince, gave his directions accordingly. For whereas the one encouraged the social intercourse of the priests of God, desiring thus to honor Him whom they served, and with a view to peace and unity of judgment; the other, whose object it was to destroy everything that was good, used all his endeavors to bring discord into the general harmony.

CHAPTER LII
BANISHMENT OF THE CHRISTIANS, WITH CONFISCATION AND SALE OF THEIR PROPERTY.

And whereas Constantine, the friend of God, had granted to His worshippers freedom of access to the imperial palaces, His enemy, in a spirit the very reverse of this, expelled thence all Christians subject to his authority. He banished those who had proved themselves his most faithful and devoted servants, and compelled others, on whom he had himself conferred honor and distinction as a reward for their former eminent services, to the performance of menial offices as slaves to others. And at length, being bent on seizing the property of all as his prey, he even threatened with death those who professed the Savior's name. Moreover, being himself of a nature hopelessly debased by sensuality, and degraded by the continual practice of adultery and other shameless vices, he assumed his own worthless character as a specimen of human nature generally, and denied that the virtue of chastity and continence existed among men.

CHAPTER LIII
LICINIUS'S EDICT THAT WOMEN AND MEN SHOULD NOT BE PERMITTED TO FREQUENT THE CHURCHES IN COMPANY.

Accordingly he passed a second law, which enjoined that men should not appear in company with women in the houses of prayer, and forbade women to attend the sacred schools of virtue, or to receive instruction from the bishops, directing the appointment of women to be teachers of their own sex. These regulations being received with general ridicule, he devised other means for effecting the ruin of the churches. He ordered that the usual congregations of the people should be held in the open country outside the gates, alleging that the open air without the city was far more suitable for a multitude than the houses of prayer within the walls.

CHAPTER LIV

HE DISMISSES THOSE WHO REFUSE TO SACRIFICE FROM MILITARY SERVICE, AND FORBIDS THE SUPPLY OF NECESSARY FOOD TO THOSE IN PRISON.

Failing, however, to obtain obedience in this respect also, at length he threw off the mask, and gave orders that those who held military commissions in the several cities of the empire should be deprived of their respective commands, in case of their refusal to offer sacrifices to the demons. Accordingly the forces of the authorities in every province suffered the loss of those who worshipped God, and he too who had decreed this order suffered loss, in that he thus deprived himself of the prayers of pious men. And why should I still further mention how he directed that no one should obey the dictates of common humanity by distributing food to those who were pining in prisons, or should even pity the captives who perished with hunger—in short, that no one should perform a virtuous action, and that those whose natural feelings impelled them to sympathize with their fellow-creatures, should be prohibited from doing them a single kindness? Truly this was the most utterly shameless and scandalous of all laws, and one which surpassed the worst depravity of human nature: a law which inflicted on those who shewed mercy the same penalties as on those who were the objects of their compassion, and visited the exercise of mere humanity with the severest punishments.

CHAPTER LV

THE LAWLESS CONDUCT AND COVETOUSNESS
OF LICINIUS.

Such were the ordinances of Licinius. But why should I enumerate his innovations respecting marriage, or those which had in view the property of the dying, whereby he presumed to abrogate the ancient and wisely established laws of the Romans, and to introduce certain barbarous and cruel institutions in their stead, inventing a thousand pretences for oppressing his subjects? Hence it was that he devised a new method of measuring land, by which he reckoned the smallest portion at more than its actual dimensions, from an insatiable desire of unjust exaction. Hence too he registered the names of country residents who were now no more, and had long been numbered with the dead, procuring to himself by this expedient a sordid and unlawful gain. For his meanness was as unlimited as his rapacity was insatiable. So that when he had filled all his treasuries with gold, and silver, and boundless wealth, he bitterly bewailed his poverty, and suffered as it were the torments of Tantalus. But why should I mention how many innocent persons he punished with exile; how much property he confiscated; how many men of noble birth and unblemished character he imprisoned, whose wives he handed over to be basely insulted by his profligate slaves; in short, to how many married women and virgins he himself offered violence, though already feeling the infirmities of age? I need not enlarge on these subjects, since the enormity of his last actions causes the former to appear trifling and of little moment.

CHAPTER LVI

AT LENGTH HE UNDERTAKES TO RAISE
A PERSECUTION AGAINST THE CHRISTIANS.

For the final efforts of his fury appeared in his open hostility to the churches. And he directed his attacks against the bishops themselves, whom he regarded as his worst adversaries, bearing special enmity to a class of men whom the great and pious emperor treated as his friends. Accordingly he spent on us the utmost of his fury, and, being transported beyond the bounds of reason, he paused not to reflect on the example of those who had persecuted the Christians before him, nor of those whom he himself had been raised up to punish and destroy for their impious deeds. Nor did he heed the facts of which he had been himself a witness, though he had seen with his own eyes the chief originator of these our calamities (whoever he was),[23] smitten by the stroke of Divine vengeance.

CHAPTER LVII

MAXIMIAN, BROUGHT LOW BY A FISTULOUS
ULCER WITH WORMS, ISSUES AN EDICT
IN FAVOR OF THE CHRISTIANS.

For whereas this man had commenced the attack on the churches, and had been the first to pollute his soul with the blood of just and godly men, a judgment from God overtook him, which at first affected his body, but eventually extended itself to his soul. For suddenly an abscess appeared in the secret parts of his person, followed by a deeply seated fistulous ulcer; and these diseases fastened with incurable virulence on the intestines, which swarmed with a vast multitude of worms, and emitted a pestilential odor. Besides, his entire person had become loaded, through gluttonous excess, with an enormous quantity of fat, and this, being now in a putrescent state, is said to have presented to all who approached him an intolerable and dreadful spectacle. Having, therefore, to struggle against such sufferings, at length, though late, he became conscience-stricken on account of his past crimes against the Church, and, confessing his sins before God, he put a stop to the persecution of the Christians, and hastened to issue imperial edicts and rescripts for the rebuilding of their churches, at the same time enjoining them to perform their customary worship, and to offer up prayers on his behalf.

CHAPTER LVIII

HOW MAXIMIN, WHO HAD PERSECUTED THE CHRISTIANS, WAS COMPELLED TO FLY, AND CONCEAL HIMSELF IN THE DISGUISE OF A SLAVE.

Such was the punishment which he underwent who had commenced the persecution. Licinius, however, of whom we were just now speaking, who had been a witness of these things, and known them by his own actual experience, banished the remembrance of them altogether from his mind, and reflected neither on the punishment of the first, nor the divine judgment which had been executed on the second persecutor.[24] The latter had indeed endeavored to outstrip his predecessor in the career of crime, and prided himself on the invention of new tortures for us. Not content with tormenting his victims by fire and sword, piercing them with nails, or destroying them by the fangs of wild beasts or in the depths of the sea, in addition to all these, he discovered a new and strange mode of punishment, and issued an edict directing that they should be partially bereft of sight. So that numbers, not of men only, but of women and children, after being deprived of the sight of their eyes, and the use of the joints of their feet, by mutilation or cautery, were consigned in this condition to the painful labor of the mines. Hence it was that this tyrant also was overtaken not long after by the righteous judgment of God, at a time when, confiding in the aid of the demons whom he worshipped as his gods, and relying on the countless multitudes of his troops, he had ventured to engage in battle. For, feeling himself on that occasion destitute of all hope in God, he threw from him the imperial dress which so ill became him, hid himself with unmanly timidity in the crowd around him, and sought safety in flight. He afterwards lurked about the fields and villages in the habit of a slave, hoping he should thus be effectually concealed. He had not, however, eluded the mighty and all-searching gaze of God. For even while he was expecting to pass the residue of his days in security, he fell prostrate, smitten by God's fiery dart, and his whole body withered by the stroke of Divine vengeance, so that all trace of the original lineaments of his person was lost, and nothing remained to him but dry and parched bones, presenting the appearance of a lifeless image.

CHAPTER LIX
MAXIMIN, BLINDED BY MEANS OF HIS DISEASE, ISSUES AN ORDINANCE IN FAVOR OF THE CHRISTIANS.

And still the stroke of God continued heavy upon him, so that his eyes protruded and fell from their sockets, leaving him quite blind: and thus he suffered, by a most righteous retribution, the very same punishment which he had been the first to devise for the martyrs of God. At length, however (for he survived—even these sufferings), he too implored pardon of the God of the Christians, and confessed his impious opposition of the will of heaven. He too recanted, as the former persecutor had done, and by laws and ordinances explicitly acknowledged his error in worshipping those whom he had accounted gods, declaring that he now knew, by positive experience, that the God of the Christians was the only true God. These were facts which Licinius had not merely received on the testimony of others, but of which he had himself had personal knowledge. And yet, as though his understanding had been obscured by some dark cloud of error, he resolved to persist in the same evil course.

NOTES

1. In the text it is ὁ λόγος, "my power of speech, or of description, much desires," and so throughout this preface: but this kind of personification seems scarcely suited to the English idiom.

2. Κηροχύτου γραφῆς, properly, encaustic painting, by means of melted wax.

3. Γιγάντων. The persecuting emperors appear to be meant, of whom there is more mention hereafter.

4. Such seems to be the probable meaning of this passage, which is manifestly corrupt, and of which various emendations have been proposed.

5. *Note to the 2009 edition:* Constantine is also compared to Alexander as well as other Roman Emperors in *The Cæsars* composed by his nephew, Julian 'the Apostate,' Emperor from AD 361–363. A devout pagan, Julian reviled his uncle as a profligate and derided his achievements as "mere gardens of Adonis." (see *The Works of the Emperor Julian,* Vol. II, p. 399).

6. Alluding probably to Ecclesiastes 11:28, "Judge none blessed before his death; for a man shall be known in his children." Or, possibly, to the well-known opinion of Solon to the same effect. See Herod. 1. 32: Aristot. Eth. Nicom. 1. 11.

7. Diocletian, Maximian, Galerius, and Constantius.

8. *Note to the 2009 edition:* Lactantius claims that Constantius I did indeed allow churches to be destroyed in accordance with the orders of the senior emperors, but otherwise did no harm to the Christians under his rule. (see *De Mortibus Persecutorum,* p. 23).

9. *Note to the 2009 edition:* Eutropius generally agrees with Eusebius's

assessment of Constantius I, calling him, "an outstanding man and exceptionally gracious." He also confirms the personal austerity of Constantius and his beloved reputation among the people of Gaul (*Breviarum*, p. 64).

10. *Note to the 2009 edition:* A more detailed account of Constantine's ill-treatment and escape from Galerius (Not Diocletian as indicated in the title of Chapter XX), may be found in Lactantius, *De Mortibus Persecutorum*, p. 39).

11. Eusebius here speaks of a second expedition of Constantine to Britain, which is not mentioned by other ancient writers; or he may have been forgetful or ignorant of the fact that Constantine had received the imperial authority in Britain itself, Constantius having died in his palace at York, AD 306.

12. *Note to the 2009 edition:* For the failures of Galerius to overthrow the usurper Maxentius, see Lactantius, *De Mortibus Persecutorum*, p. 41–43.

13. *Note to the 2009 edition:* Though the passage concerning the miracle of the cross is unique to Eusebius, the account of Constantine's dream about the labarum is corroborated by Lactantius (See *De Mortibus Persecutorum*, p. 63).

14. From the Bretagnic *lab*, to raise, or, from *labarva*, which, in the Basque language, still signifies a standard—Riddle's Lat. Dict. *voc.* Labarum. Gibbon declares the derivation and meaning of the word to be "totally unknown, in spite of the efforts of the critics, who have ineffectually tortured the Latin, Greek, Spanish, Celtic, Teutonic, Illyric, Armenian, etc., in search of an etymology." See Gibbon, *Decline and Fall*, chap. xx, note 33.

15. Χιαζομένου τοῦ ῥ κατὰ τὸ μεσαίτατον. The figure ☧ would seem to answer to the description in the text. Gibbon gives two specimens ⚑ and ☧, as engraved from ancient monuments. Chap. xx, note 35.

16. Psalms 7:15, 16.

17. *Note to the 2009 edition:* For additional details about the Battle of the Milvian Bridge, see Lactantius, *De Mortibus Persecutorum*, p. 65, Aurelius Victor, *De Cæsaribus*, p. 48, Zosimus, *New History*, p. 43–44.

18. Exodus 15:1, 2, 11.

19. Unless Φωνῇ τε μεγάλῃ be the true reading.

20. This passage in the text is defective or corrupt.

21. *Note to the 2009 edition:* Eusebius refers here to Maximian Herculius, the colleague of Diocletian and the father of Maxentius. Lactantius provides a fuller account of the intrigues and death of Maximian. See *De Mortibus Persecutorum*, p. 43–47.

22. The Bishops.
23. Galerius Maximian. The description of his illness and death in the next chapter is repeated from the author's *Ecclesiastical History*, lib. viii. c 16; English Translation, page 277–278.
24. Maximin, ruler of the Eastern provinces of the empire. Also known as Maximinus Daia.

BOOK II

CHAPTER I

SECRET PERSECUTION BY LICINIUS, WHO CAUSES SOME BISHOPS TO BE PUT TO DEATH AT AMASIA OF PONTUS.

In this manner, he of whom we have spoken, continued to rush headlong towards that destruction which awaits the enemies of God, and once more, with a fatal emulation of their example whose ruin he had himself witnessed as the consequence of their impious conduct, he re-kindled the persecution of the Christians, like a long extinguished fire, and fanned the unhallowed flame to a fiercer height than any who had gone before him.

At first, indeed, though breathing fury and threatenings against God, like some savage beast of prey, or some closely coiled and crafty serpent, he dared not, from fear of Constantine, openly level his attacks against the Churches of God subject to his dominion, but dissembled the virulence of his malice, and endeavored by secret measures, limited in the sphere of their operation, to compass the death of the bishops, the most eminent of whom he found means to remove, through charges laid against them by the governors of the several provinces. And the manner in which they suffered had in it something strange, and hitherto unheard of. At all events, the barbarities perpetrated at Amasia of Pontus, surpassed every known excess of cruelty.

CHAPTER II
DEMOLITION OF CHURCHES, AND CRUEL
BUTCHERY OF THE BISHOPS.

For in that city some of the churches were levelled with the ground (for the second time since the commencement of the persecutions), and others were closed by the governors of the several districts, in order to prevent any who frequented them from assembling together, or rendering due worship to God. For he by whose orders these outrages were committed was too conscious of his own crimes to expect that these services were performed with any view to his benefit, and was convinced that all we did, and all our endeavors to obtain the favor of God, were on Constantine's behalf. These servile governors then, feeling assured that such a course would be pleasing to the impious tyrant, subjected the most distinguished prelates of the churches to capital punishment.

Accordingly, men who had been guilty of no crime were led away, without any reason assigned, to undergo the penalties due to murderers. And some suffered a new kind of death, having their bodies cut piecemeal into many portions, and, after this horribly cruel and more than tragic punishment, being cast, as a prey to fishes, into the depths of the sea. The result of these horrors was once more (as on a former occasion), the flight of pious men, and again the fields and deserts afforded a refuge to the worshippers of God. But further, the tyrant having thus far succeeded in his object, began to consider how he might raise a general persecution of the Christians.[1] And he would have gratified his wishes, nor could any thing have hindered him from carrying his resolution into effect, had not He who defends His own anticipated the coming evil, and by His special guidance conducted His servant Constantine to this part of the empire, causing him to shine forth as a brilliant light in the midst of the dark and gloomy shades of night.

CHAPTER III

HOW CONSTANTINE WAS MOVED WITH PITY ON BEHALF OF THE CHRISTIANS THUS IN DANGER OF PERSECUTION.

He was not long in perceiving the intolerable nature of the evils of which he had heard, and forming at once a steadfast resolution, he tempered the natural clemency of his character with a certain measure of severity and sternness, and hastened to succor those who were thus grievously oppressed. For he judged that it would rightly be deemed a pious and holy task to secure, by the removal of an individual, the safety of the greater part of the human race. He judged too, that if he listened to the dictates of clemency only, and bestowed his pity on one utterly unworthy of it, this would, on the one hand, confer no real benefit on a man whom nothing would induce to abandon his evil practices, and whose fury against his subjects would only be likely to increase, while, on the other hand, those who suffered from his oppression would thus be for ever deprived of all hope of deliverance.

Influenced by these reflections, the emperor resolved without further delay to extend a protecting hand to those who had fallen into such an extremity of distress. He accordingly made the usual warlike preparations, and assembled his whole forces, both of horse and foot. But before them all was carried the standard which I have before described, as the symbol of his full confidence in God.

CHAPTER IV

CONSTANTINE PREPARES HIMSELF FOR THE WAR BY PRAYER, LICINIUS BY THE PRACTICE OF DIVINATION.

He took with him also the priests of God, feeling well assured that now, if ever, he stood in need of the efficacy of prayer, and thinking it right that they should constantly be near and about his person, as most trusty guardians of the soul.

Now, as soon as the tyrant understood that Constantine's victories over his enemies were secured to him by no other means than the cooperation of God, and that the persons above alluded to were continually with him and about his person, and besides this, that the symbol of the salutary passion preceded both the emperor himself and his whole army, he regarded these precautions with ridicule (as might be expected), at the same time mocking and reviling the emperor with opprobrious terms.

On the other hand, he gathered round himself Egyptian diviners and soothsayers, with sorcerers and enchanters, and the priests of those whom he imagined to be gods. He then, after offering the sacrifices which he thought the occasion demanded, inquired how far he might reckon on a successful termination of the war. They replied with one voice, that he would unquestionably be victorious and triumphant in the war: and the oracles everywhere held out to him the same prospect in copious and elegant verses. The soothsayers certified him of favorable omens from the flight of birds, the priests declared the same to be indicated by the motion of the entrails of their victims. Elevated, therefore, by these fallacious assurances, he boldly advanced at the head of his army, and prepared for battle.

CHAPTER V

LICINIUS, WHILE SACRIFICING IN A GROVE, UTTERS HIS SENTIMENTS CONCERNING IDOLS, AND CONCERNING CHRIST.

And when he was now ready to engage, he desired the most approved of his body-guard and his most valued friends, to meet him in one of the places which they consider sacred. It was a well watered and shady grove, and in it were several marble statues of those whom he accounted to be gods. After lighting tapers and performing the usual sacrifices in honor of these, he is said to have delivered the following speech:—

"Friends and fellow-soldiers! These are our country's gods, and these we honor with a worship derived from our remotest ancestors. But he who leads the army now opposed to us has proved false to the religion of his forefathers, and adopted the sentiments of those who deny the existence of the gods. And yet he is so infatuated as to honor some strange and unheard-of Deity, with whose despicable standard he now disgraces his army, and confiding in whose aid he has taken up arms, and is now advancing, not so much against us as against those very gods whom he has despised. However, the present occasion shall prove which of us is mistaken in his judgment, and shall decide between our gods and those whom our adversaries profess to honor. For either it will declare the victory to be ours, and so most justly evince that our gods are the true Saviors and assistants, or else, if this God of Constantine's, who comes we know not whence, shall prove superior to our many deities (for at least ours have the advantage in point of numbers), let no one henceforth doubt which god he ought to worship, but attach himself at once to the superior power, and ascribe to him the honors of the victory. Suppose then this strange God, whom we now regard with contempt, should really prove victorious; then indeed we must acknowledge and give him honor, and so bid a long farewell to those for whom we light our tapers in vain. But if our own gods triumph (and of this there can be no real doubt), then, as soon as we have secured the present victory, let us prosecute the war without delay against these despisers of the gods."

Such were the words he addressed to those then present, as reported not long after to the writer of this history by some who heard them spoken, And as soon as he had concluded his speech, he gave orders to his forces to commence the attack.

CHAPTER VI

AN APPARITION SEEN IN THE CITIES SUBJECT TO LICINIUS, AS OF CONSTANTINE'S VICTORIOUS TROOPS PASSING THROUGH THEM

About this time a supernatural appearance is said to have been observed in the cities subject to the tyrant's rule. Different detachments of Constantine's army seemed to present themselves to the view, marching at noonday through these cities, as though they had obtained the victory. In reality, not a single soldier was any where present at the time, and yet this appearance was seen through the agency of a divine and superior power: and it was a vision which foreshadowed what was shortly coming to pass. For as soon as the armies were ready to engage, he who had broken through the ties of friendly alliance[2] was the first to commence the battle, on which Constantine, calling on the name of "God the Supreme Savior," and giving this as the watchword to his soldiers, overcame him in this first conflict. And not long after in a second battle he gained a still more important and decisive victory, for on this occasion the salutary trophy preceded the ranks of his army.

CHAPTER VII

VICTORY EVERYWHERE FOLLOWS
THE PRESENCE OF THE STANDARD
OF THE CROSS IN BATTLE.

Indeed, wherever this appeared, the enemy soon fled before his victorious troops. And the emperor perceiving this, whenever he saw any part of his forces hard pressed, gave orders that the salutary trophy should be moved in that direction, like some triumphant and effectual remedy against disasters. The combatants were divinely inspired, as it were, with fresh strength and courage, and immediate victory was the result.

CHAPTER VIII

FIFTY MEN ARE SELECTED TO CARRY THE CROSS.

Accordingly, he selected those of his bodyguard who were most distinguished for personal strength, valor, and piety, and intrusted them with the sole care and defense of the standard. They were in number not less than fifty, and their only duty was to surround and vigilantly defend the standard, which they carried each in turn on their shoulders. These circumstances were related to the writer of this narrative by the emperor himself in his leisure moments, long after the occurrence of the events, and he added another incident well worthy of being recorded.

CHAPTER IX

ONE OF THE CROSS-BEARERS WHO FLED FROM HIS POST IS SLAIN, WHILE ANOTHER WHO FAITHFULLY STOOD HIS GROUND IS PRESERVED.

For he said that once, during the very heat of an engagement, a sudden tumult and panic attacked his army, which threw the soldier who then bore the standard into an agony of fear, so that he handed it over to another, in order to secure his own escape from the battle. As soon, however, as his comrade had received it, and he had withdrawn, and resigned all charge of the standard, he was struck in the belly by a dart, and lost his life. Thus he paid the penalty of his cowardice and unfaithfulness, and lay dead on the spot. But the other who had taken his place as the bearer of the salutary standard, found it to be the safeguard of his life. For though he was assailed by a continual shower of darts, the bearer remained unhurt, the staff of the standard receiving every weapon. It was indeed a truly marvellous circumstance, that the enemies' darts all fell within and remained in the slender circumference of this spear, and thus saved the standard-bearer from death, so that none of those engaged in this service ever received a wound.

This story is none of mine, but for this[3] too I am indebted to the emperor's own authority, who related it in my hearing along with other matters. And now, having thus through the power of God secured these first victories, he put his forces in motion and continued his onward march.

CHAPTER X
VARIOUS BATTLES, AND CONSTANTINE'S VICTORIES.

The van, however, of the enemy, unable to resist the emperor's first assault, threw down their arms, and prostrated themselves at his feet. All these experienced his clemency, and he joyfully embraced the opportunity of sparing human life. But there were others who still continued in arms, and prepared to hazard the event of a battle. Against these the emperor, after vainly endeavoring to conciliate them by friendly overtures, ordered his army to commence the attack. On this they immediately turned and betook themselves to flight; and some were overtaken and slain according to the laws of war, while others fell on each other in the confusion of their flight, and perished by the swords of their comrades.[4]

CHAPTER XI
FLIGHT AND MAGIC ARTS OF LICINIUS.

In these circumstances their commander, finding himself bereft of the aid of his followers, having lost his lately numerous array, both of regular and allied forces, having proved too, by experience, how vain his confidence had been in false gods, was fain to submit to the disgrace of an ignominious flight, by which he effected his escape, and secured his personal safety. For the pious emperor had forbidden his soldiers to follow him too closely, and thus allowed him an opportunity for escape. And this he did in the hope that he might hereafter, on conviction of the desperate state of his affairs, be induced to abandon his insane and presumptuous ambition, and assume a more reasonable tone of temper and conduct. Such were the thoughts which Constantine's extreme humanity prompted, and such his willingness patiently to bear past injuries, and extend his forgiveness to one who so ill deserved it.

Licinius, however, far from renouncing his evil practices, still added crime to crime, and ventured on more daring atrocities than ever. Nay, he once more attempted to raise his courage by tampering with the detestable arts of magic, so that it might well be said of him, as it was of the Egyptian tyrant of old, that God had hardened his heart.

CHAPTER XII

CONSTANTINE, AFTER PRAYING IN HIS TABERNACLE, OBTAINS THE VICTORY.

In this manner Licinius gave himself up to these impieties, and rushed blindly towards the gulf of destruction. But as soon as the emperor was aware that he must meet his enemies in a second battle, he applied himself with earnestness to the worship of his Savior. He pitched the tabernacle of the cross[5] outside and at a distance from his camp, and there passed his time in pure and holy seclusion, and in offering up prayers to God, following thus the example of His ancient prophet, of whom the sacred oracles testify, that he pitched the tabernacle without the camp.[6] He was attended only by a few, of whose faith and piety, as well as affection to his person, he was well assured. And this custom he continued to observe whenever he meditated an engagement with the enemy. For he was deliberate in his measures, the better to insure safety, and desired in everything to be directed by divine counsel. And since his prayers ascended with fervor and earnestness to God, he was always honored with a manifestation of His presence. And then, as if moved by a divine impulse, he would rush from the tabernacle, and suddenly give orders to his army to move at once without delay, and on the instant to draw their swords. On this they would immediately commence the attack, with great and general slaughter, so as with incredible celerity to secure the victory, and raise trophies in token of the overthrow of their enemies.

CHAPTER XIII
HIS HUMANE TREATMENT OF PRISONERS.

To such exercises as these the emperor had long accustomed both himself and his army, whenever there was a prospect of an engagement, for his God was ever present to his thoughts, and he desired to do everything according to His will. He had also a pious abhorrence of any wanton sacrifice of human life, which induced him to be anxious for the preservation not only of his own subjects, but even of his enemies. Accordingly he directed his victorious troops to spare the lives of their prisoners, admonishing them, as human beings, not to forget the claims of their common nature. And whenever he saw the passions of his soldiery excited beyond the limits of self-control, he repressed their fury by a largess of money, rewarding every man who saved the life of an enemy with a certain weight of gold. Constantine's own sagacity led him to discover this inducement to spare human life, and great numbers even of the barbarians were thus saved, and owed their lives to the emperor's gold.

CHAPTER XIV
A FURTHER MENTION OF HIS PRAYERS
IN THE TABERNACLE.

Now these, and a thousand such acts as these, were familiarly and habitually practiced by the emperor. But on the present occasion he retired (as his custom was before battle) to the privacy of his tabernacle, and there employed himself in earnest prayer to God. Meanwhile he strictly abstained from anything like levity of spirit, or luxurious living, and disciplined himself by fasting and bodily mortification, imploring the favor of God by supplication and prayer, that he might obtain His concurrence and aid, and be ready to execute whatever He might be pleased to suggest to his thoughts. In short, he exercised an unceasing care and watchfulness over all alike, and interceded with God as much for the safety of his enemies as for that of his own subjects.

CHAPTER XV

PRETENDED FRIENDSHIP AND IDOLATROUS PRACTICES OF LICINIUS.

And inasmuch as he who had lately fled before him now dissembled his real sentiments, and again petitioned for a renewal of friendship and alliance, the emperor thought fit, on certain conditions, to grant his request,[7] in the hope that such a measure might be expedient, and generally advantageous to the community. Licinius, however, while he pretended a ready submission to the terms prescribed, and attested his sincerity by oaths, at this very time was secretly engaged in collecting a military force, and again meditated war and strife, inviting even the barbarians to join his standard.[8] He began also to look about him for other gods, having been deceived by those in whom he had hitherto trusted, and, without bestowing a thought on what he had himself publicly spoken on the subject of false deities, or choosing to acknowledge that God who had fought on the side of Constantine, he made himself ridiculous by seeking for a multitude of new gods.

CHAPTER XVI

LICINIUS CHARGES HIS SOLDIERS NOT TO ATTACK THE STANDARD OF THE CROSS.

Having by this time had full proof of the Divine and mysterious power which resided in the salutary trophy, by means of which Constantine's army had become habituated to victory, he admonished his soldiers never to direct their attack against this standard, nor even incautiously to allow their eyes to rest upon it, assuring them that it possessed a terrible power, and was especially hostile to him, so that they would do well carefully to avoid any collision with it. And now, having given these directions, he prepared for a decisive conflict with him whose humanity prompted him still to hesitate, and to postpone the fate which he foresaw awaited his adversary. The enemy, however, confident in the aid of a multitude of gods, advanced to the attack with a powerful array of military force, preceded by certain images of the dead, and lifeless statues, as their defense. On the other side, the emperor, secure in the armor of godliness, opposed to the numbers of the enemy the salutary and life-giving sign, as at once a terror to the foe, and a protection from every harm. And for a while he paused, and preserved at first the attitude of forbearance, from respect to the treaty of peace to which he had given his sanction, that he might not be the first to commence the contest.

CHAPTER XVII

CONSTANTINE'S VICTORY.

But as soon as he perceived that his adversaries persisted in their resolution, and were already drawing their swords, he gave free scope to his indignation, and by a single charge overthrew in a moment the entire body of the enemy, thus triumphing at once over them and the evil spirits whom they served.

CHAPTER XVIII

DEATH OF LICINIUS, AND CONSEQUENT TRIUMPH.

He then proceeded to deal with this adversary of God and his followers according to the laws of war, and consign them to the fate which their crimes deserved. Accordingly the tyrant himself, and they whose counsels had supported him in his impiety, were together subjected to the just punishment of death. After this, those who had so lately been deceived by their vain confidence in false deities, acknowledged with unfeigned sincerity the God of Constantine, and openly professed their belief in Him as the true and only God.

CHAPTER XIX

GENERAL REJOICINGS.

And now, the impious being thus removed, the sun once more shone brightly after the gloomy cloud of tyrannic power. Each separate portion of the Roman dominion became blended with the rest; the Eastern nations united with those of the West, and the whole body of the Roman empire was graced as it were by its head in the person of a single and supreme ruler, whose authority pervaded the whole. Now too the bright rays of the light of godliness gladdened the days of those who had heretofore been sitting in darkness and the shadow of death. Past sorrows were no more remembered, for all united in celebrating the praises of the victorious prince, and avowed their recognition of his preserver as the only true God. Thus our emperor, whose character shone with all the graces of religion, with the title of Victor (for he had himself adopted this name as a most fitting appellation to express the victory which God had granted him over all who hated or opposed him), assumed the dominion of the East, and thus singly governed the Roman empire, re-united, as in former times, under one head. Thus, as he was the first to proclaim to all the sole sovereignty of God, so he himself, as monarch of the Roman world, extended his authority over the whole human race. Every apprehension of those evils under the pressure of which all had suffered was now removed: men whose heads had drooped in sorrow now regarded each other with smiling countenances, and looks expressive of their inward joy. And first of all, with processions and hymns of praise they ascribed the supreme sovereignty to God, as in truth the King of kings; and then with continued acclamations rendered honor to the victorious emperor, and the Cæsars, his most discreet and pious sons. The former afflictions were forgotten, and all past impieties forgiven, while with the enjoyment of present happiness was mingled the expectation of still future blessings.

CHAPTER XX

CONSTANTINE'S ENACTMENTS IN FAVOR OF THE CONFESSORS.

Moreover, the emperor's humane and benignant edicts were published among us also, as they had been among the inhabitants of the western division of the empire. And his laws, which breathed a spirit of piety toward God, gave promise of manifold blessings, since they secured many advantages to his provincial subjects in every nation, and at the same time prescribed measures suited to the exigencies of the churches of God. For first of all they recalled those who, in consequence of their refusal to join in idol worship, had been driven to exile, or ejected from their homes by the governors of their respective provinces. In the next place, they relieved from their burdens those who for the same reason had been adjudged to serve in the civil courts, and ordained restitution to be made to any who had been deprived of property. They too, who in the time of trial had signalized themselves by fortitude of soul in the cause of God, and had therefore been condemned to the dreadful labor of the mines, or consigned to the solitude of islands, or compelled to toil in the public works, all received an absolute release from these burdens; while others, whose religious constancy had cost them the forfeiture of their military rank, were vindicated by the emperor's generosity from this dishonor. For he granted them the alternative either of resuming their rank, and enjoying their former privileges, or (in the event of their preferring a more settled life), of perpetual exemption from all service, Lastly, all who had been compelled by way of disgrace and insult to serve in the employments of women,[9] obtained an equal emancipation with the rest.

CHAPTER XXI

HIS LAWS IN FAVOR OF MARTYRS, AND RESPECTING THE PROPERTY OF THE CHURCHES.

Such were the benefits secured by the emperor's written mandates to the persons of those who had thus suffered for the faith; and his laws made ample provision for their property also.

With regard to those holy martyrs of God who had laid down their lives in the confession of His name, he directed that their estates should be enjoyed by their nearest kindred, and, in default of any of these, that the right of inheritance should be vested in the churches. Further, whatever property had been consigned to other parties from the treasury, whether in the way of sale or gift, together with that retained in the treasury itself, the generous mandate of the emperor directed should be restored to the original owners. Such benefits did his bounty, thus widely diffused, confer on the Church of God.

CHAPTER XXII

HOW HE CHERISHED THE INTERESTS OF THE SEVERAL NATIONS OF HIS EMPIRE.

But his munificence bestowed still further and more numerous favors on the heathen tribes and other nations of his empire. So that the inhabitants of our Eastern regions (who had heard of the privileges experienced in the opposite portion of the empire, and had blessed the fortunate recipients of them, and longed for the enjoyment of a similar lot for themselves), now with one consent proclaimed their own happiness, when they saw themselves in possession of all these blessings, and confessed that the appearance of such a monarch to the human race was indeed a marvellous event, and such as the world's history had never yet recorded. Such were the sentiments which animated their breasts.

CHAPTER XXIII

HOW HE DECLARED GOD TO BE THE AUTHOR OF HIS PROSPERITY, AND CONCERNING HIS WRITTEN LAWS.

And now that (through the powerful aid of God his Savior), all nations owned their subjection to the emperor's authority, he openly proclaimed to all the name of Him to whose bounty he owed all his blessings, and declared that He, and not himself, was the author of his past victories. This declaration, written both in the Latin and Greek languages, he caused to be transmitted through every province of the empire. Now the excellence of his style of expression may be known from a perusal of his letters himself which were two in number—one addressed to the churches of God, the other to the heathen population in the several cities of the empire. The latter of these I think it well to insert here, as connected with my present subject, in order on the one hand that a copy of this document may be recorded as matter of history, and thus preserved to posterity, and on the other that it may serve to confirm the truth of my present narrative. It is taken from an authentic copy of the imperial statute in my own possession, and the signature in the emperor's own handwriting attaches as it were the impress of truth to the statement I have made.

CHAPTER XXIV

LAW OF CONSTANTINE RESPECTING PIETY TOWARDS GOD, AND THE CHRISTIAN RELIGION.[10]

Victor Constantinus, Maximus Augustus, to the inhabitants of the province of Palestine.

To all who entertain just and wise sentiments respecting the character of the Supreme Being, it has long been most clearly evident, and beyond the possibility of doubt, how vast a difference there has ever been between those who maintain a careful observance of the hallowed duties of the Christian religion, and those who treat this religion with hostility or contempt. But at this present time, we may see by still more manifest proofs, and still more decisive instances, both how unreasonable it were to question this truth, and how mighty is the power of the Supreme God—since it, appears that they who faithfully observe His holy laws, and shrink from the transgression of His commandments, are rewarded with abundant blessings, and are endued with well-grounded hope as well as ample power for the accomplishment of their undertakings. On the other hand, they who have cherished impious sentiments have experienced results corresponding to their evil choice. For how is it to be expected that any blessing would be obtained by one who neither desired to acknowledge nor duly to worship that God who is the source of all blessing? Indeed, facts themselves are a confirmation of what I say.

But besides this, whoever will mentally retrace the course of events from the earliest period down to the present time, and allow himself to reflect on what has occurred in past ages, will find that all who have made justice and probity the basis of their conduct, have not only carried their undertakings to a successful issue, but have gathered as it were a store of sweet fruit as the produce of this pleasant root. Again, whoever observes the career of those who have been bold in the practice of oppression or injustice, who have either directed their senseless fury against God Himself, or have conceived no kindly feelings towards their fellow men, but have dared to afflict them with exile, disgrace, confiscation, massacre, or other miseries of the like kind (and all this without any sense of compunction, or wish to direct their thoughts to a better course), will find that such men have received a recompense proportioned to their crimes. And these are results which might naturally and reasonably be expected to ensue.

For whoever have addressed themselves with integrity of purpose to any course of action, keeping the fear of God continually before their thoughts, and holding fast an unwavering faith in Him, without allowing present fears or dangers to outweigh their hope of future blessings, such persons, though for a season they may have experienced painful trials, have borne their afflictions lightly, being supported by the belief of greater rewards in store for them. And their character has acquired a brighter luster in proportion to the severity of their past sufferings. With regard, on the other hand, to those who have either foully slighted the principles of justice, or refused to acknowledge the Supreme God themselves, and yet have dared to subject others who have faithfully maintained His worship to the most cruel insults and punishments—who have failed equally to recognize their own vileness in oppressing others on such grounds, and the happiness and blessing of those who preserved their devotion to God even in the midst of such sufferings—with regard, I say, to such men, many a time have their armies been slaughtered, many a time have they been put to flight, and their warlike preparations have ended in total ruin and defeat.

From the causes I have described, grievous wars arose, and destructive devastations. Hence followed a scarcity of the common necessaries of life, and a crowd of consequent miseries. Hence, too, the authors of these impieties have either terminated the extremity of suffering by a disastrous death, or have dragged out an ignominious existence, and confessed it to be worse than death itself, thus receiving as it were a measure of punishment proportioned to the heinousness of their crimes. For each experienced a degree of calamity according to the blind fury with which he had been led to combat, and (as he thought) defeat the Divine will, so that they not only felt the pressure of the ills which could reach them in this present life, but were tormented also by a most lively apprehension of punishment in a future world.

And now, with such a mass of impiety pervading the human race, and the commonwealth in danger of being utterly destroyed, as if by the agency of some pestilential disease, and therefore needing powerful and effectual aid, what was the relief, and what the remedy which God devised for these evils? (I need not say that we are to understand Him who is alone and truly God, the possessor of almighty and eternal power: and surely it cannot be deemed arrogance in one who has received benefits from God, to acknowledge them in the loftiest terms of praise). I myself, then, was the instrument whose services He chose, and esteemed suited for the accomplishment of His will. Accordingly, beginning at the remote Britannic ocean, and the regions where the sun sinks beneath the horizon in obedience to the law of nature, through the aid of divine power I banished and utterly removed every form of evil which prevailed, in the hope that the human race, enlightened through my instrumentality, might be recalled to a due observance of the holy laws of God, and at, the same time our most blessed faith might prosper under the guidance of His almighty hand. For I would desire never to be forgetful of the gratitude due to His grace.

Believing, therefore, that this most excellent

service had been confided to me as a special gift, I proceeded as far as the regions of the East, which, being under the pressure of severer calamities, seemed to demand still more effectual remedies at my hands. At the same time I am most certainly persuaded that I myself owe my life, my every breath, in short, my very inmost and secret thoughts, entirely to the favor of the Supreme God. Now I am well aware that they who are sincere in the pursuit of the heavenly hope, and have fixed this hope in heaven itself as the peculiar and predominant principle of their lives, have no need to depend on human friendship, but rather have enjoyed a higher degree of dignity in proportion as they have separated themselves from the vices and evils of this earthly existence. Nevertheless I deem it incumbent on me to remove at once and most completely from all such persons the hard necessities laid upon them for a season, and the cruel and unjust inflictions under which they have suffered, though free from any stain of guilt, For it would be strange indeed, that the fortitude and constancy of soul displayed by such men should be fully apparent during the reign of those whose first object it was to persecute them on account of their devotion to God, and yet that the glory of their character should receive no accession of luster, and be viewed in no more exalted light, under the administration of a prince who is His servant.

Let all therefore who have exchanged their country for a foreign land, because they dared not abandon that reverence and faith toward God to which they had devoted themselves with their whole hearts, and have in consequence at different times been subject to the cruel sentence of the judge, together with any who have been enrolled in the registers of the public courts, though in time past exempt from such office, let these, I say, now render thanks to God the Liberator of all, in that they are restored to their hereditary property, and the tranquility they once enjoyed. Let those also who have been despoiled of their goods, and have hitherto passed a wretched existence, mourning under the loss of all that they possessed, once more return to their former homes, their families, and estates, and receive with joy these proofs of the bountiful kindness of God.

Furthermore, it is our command that all those who have been detained in the islands against their will should receive the benefit of this present provision, in order that they who till now have been surrounded by impassable mountains and the encircling barrier of the ocean, being now set free from that frightful and dreary solitude, may fulfill the fondest wishes of their hearts by revisiting their dearest friends. Those, too, who have prolonged a miserable life in the midst of abject and loathsome wretchedness, welcoming their restoration as an unlooked-for gain, and discarding henceforth all anxious thoughts, may pass their lives with us in freedom from all fear. For that any one could live in a state of fear under our government, whose glory it is to feel confident that we are the servant of God, would surely be a thing most absurd even to hear of, far more to believe as true; since the natural desire of our heart would be completely to rectify the errors of our predecessors in this respect.

Again, with regard to those who have been

condemned either to the grievous labor of the mines, or to service in the public works, let them enjoy the sweets of leisure in place of these long continued toils, and henceforth lead a far easier life, and more accordant with the wishes of their hearts, exchanging the incessant hardships of their tasks for a pleasing and quiet rest. And if any have forfeited the common privilege of liberty, or have unhappily fallen under any mark of infamy, let them hasten back every one to the country of his nativity, and resume with becoming joy their former positions in society, from which they have been as it were estranged by long absence in a foreign land.

Once more, with respect to those who had previously been preferred to any military distinction, which they were afterwards deprived, for the cruel and unjust reason that they chose rather to acknowledge their allegiance to God than to retain the rank they held, we leave them perfect liberty of choice, either to occupy their former stations, should they be content again to engage in military service, or to live in undisturbed tranquillity, with an honorable discharge from all duty. For it is fair and reasonable that men who have displayed such magnanimity and fortitude in meeting the perils to which they have been exposed, should be allowed the choice either of enjoying peaceful leisure, or resuming their former rank.

Lastly, if any have wrongfully been deprived of the privileges of noble lineage, and subjected to a judicial sentence which has consigned them to the women's apartments for weaving or spinning, there to undergo a cruel and miserable labor, or reduced them to servitude for the benefit of the public treasury, without any exemption on the ground of superior birth, let such persons, resuming the honors they had previously enjoyed, and their proper dignities, henceforward exult in the blessings of liberty, and lead a life of happiness and joy. Let the free man,[11] too, whom the unjust and inhuman fury of his persecutors has made a slave, who has felt the sudden and mournful transition from liberty to bondage, and ofttimes bewailed his unwonted labors, return to his family once more a free man in virtue of this our ordinance, and seek those employments which befit a state of freedom. And let him dismiss from his remembrance those services which he found so oppressive, and which so ill became his condition.

Nor must we omit to notice those estates of which individuals have been deprived on various pretences. For if any of those who have engaged with dauntless resolution in the noble and divine conflict of martyrdom, have also been stripped of their fortunes, or if the same has been the lot of the confessors, who have won for themselves the hope of eternal treasures, or if the loss of property has befallen those who were driven from their native land because they could not yield that obedience to the will of their persecutors which involved a betrayal of their faith, lastly, if any who have escaped the sentence of death have yet been despoiled of their worldly goods, we ordain that the inheritances of all such persons be transferred to their nearest kindred. And whereas the laws expressly assign this right to those most nearly related, it will be easy to ascertain to whom these inheritances severally belong. And it is evidently reasonable that the succession in these cases should belong to those who would have stood in the place of nearest affinity, had the deceased experienced a natural death.

But should there be no surviving relation to succeed in due course to the property of those abovementioned—I mean the martyrs, or confessors, or those whom a similar devotion has driven from their native soil—in such cases we ordain that the church locally nearest in each instance shall succeed to the inheritance. And surely it will be no wrong to the departed that that church should be their heir, for whose sake they have endured every extremity of suffering. We think it necessary to add this also that in case any of the above-mentioned persons have chosen to bequeath any part of their property in the way of free gift, possession of such property shall be assured (as is reasonable) to those who have thus received it.

And that there may be no apparent obscurity in this our ordinance, but everyone may readily apprehend its requirements, let all men hereby know that if they are now maintaining themselves in possession of a piece of land, or a house, or garden, or any thing else which had appertained to those persons of whom we have before spoken, it will be good and advantageous for them to acknowledge the fact, and make restitution with the least possible delay. On the other hand, although it should appear that some individuals have reaped abundant profits from this unjust possession, we do not consider that justice absolutely demands the restitution of such profits.

They must, however, declare explicitly what amount of benefit they have thus derived, and from what sources, and entreat our pardon for this offense, in order that their past covetousness may in some measure be atoned for, and that the Supreme Being may accept this compensation as a token of contrition, and be pleased graciously to pardon the sin. But it is possible that those who have become masters of such property (if it be right or possible to allow them such a title), will assure us by way of apology for their conduct, that it was not in their power to abstain from this appropriation at a time when a spectacle of misery in all its forms every where met the view—when men were cruelly driven from their homes, slaughtered without mercy, thrust forth without remorse, when the proscription of innocent persons was a common thing, when the fury of persecution was insatiable, and property seized and openly exposed for sale. If any defend their conduct by such reasons as these, and still persist in their avaricious temper, they shall be made sensible that such a course will bring punishment on themselves, and the rather so, because this correction of evil is the very characteristic of our service to the Supreme God. So that it will henceforth be dangerous to retain what dire necessity may in time past have compelled men to take; especially because it is in any case incumbent on us to discourage covetous desires, both by persuasion, and by making examples of the guilty.

Nor shall the treasury itself, should it claim a right to any of the things we have spoken of, be permitted to maintain that right, but without venturing as it were to raise its voice against the holy churches, it shall justly relinquish in their favor what it has long unjustly retained. We ordain, therefore, that all things whatsoever which shall appear really to belong to the churches (whether the property consist of houses, or fields and gardens, or whatever the nature of it may be), shall be restored in their full value and integrity, and with undiminished right of possession.

Again, with respect to those places which are honored in being the depositories of the remains of martyrs, and continue to be memorials of their glorious departure, how can we doubt that they rightly belong to the churches, or refrain from issuing our injunction to that effect? For surely there can be no better liberality, no labor more pleasing or profitable, than to be thus employed under the guidance of the Divine Spirit, in order that those rights which have been appropriated on false pretences by unjust and wicked men, may be restored, as just demands, and once more secured to the holy churches.

And since it would be wrong in a provision intended to include all cases, to pass over those who have either procured any such property by right of purchase from the treasury, or have retained it when conveyed to them in the form of a gift, let all who have thus rashly indulged their insatiable thirst of gain be assured that, although by daring to make such purchases they have done all in their power to alienate our clemency from themselves, they shall nevertheless not fail of obtaining it, so far as is possible and consistent with propriety in each case.

And now, since it appears by the clearest and most convincing evidence, that the miseries which ere while oppressed the entire human race are now banished from every part of the world, partly by the power of Almighty God, and partly by means of the counsel and aid which He is pleased on many occasions to administer through our agency, it remains for all, both individually and unitedly, to observe and seriously consider how great this power and how efficacious this grace are, which have annihilated and utterly destroyed this generation (as I may call them) of most wicked and evil men, have restored joy to the good, and diffused it over all countries, and now guarantee the fullest liberty both to honor the Divine law as it should be honored, with all reverence, and to pay due observance to those who have dedicated themselves to the service of that law, and who will now lift up their heads as it were after a period of profound darkness, and, with an enlightened knowledge of the present course of events, will henceforward render to its percepts that becoming reverence and honor which are consistent with their pious character.

Let this ordinance be published in our Eastern provinces.[12]

CHAPTER XXV

CONSTANTINE'S ENACTMENTS WERE CARRIED INTO EFFECT.

Such were the injunctions contained in the first letter which the emperor addressed to us. And the provisions of this enactment were speedily carried into effect, everything being conducted in a manner quite different from the atrocities which had but lately been daringly perpetrated during the cruel ascendancy of the tyrants. Those persons also who were legally entitled to it, received the benefit of the emperor's liberality.

CHAPTER XXVI

HE PROMOTES CHRISTIANS TO OFFICES OF GOVERNMENT, AND FORBIDS GENTILES IN SUCH STATIONS TO OFFER SACRIFICE.

After this the emperor continued to address himself to matters of high importance, and first he sent governors to the several provinces, mostly such as were devoted to the saving faith. And if any appeared inclined to adhere to Gentile worship, he forbade them to offer sacrifice. This law applied also to those who surpassed the provincial governors in rank and dignity,[13] and even to those who occupied the highest station, and held the authority of the Prætorian Prefecture.[14] If they were Christians, they were free to act consistently with their profession. If otherwise, the law required them to abstain from idolatrous sacrifices.

CHAPTER XXVII

STATUTES WHICH FORBADE SACRIFICE, AND ENJOINED THE BUILDING OF CHURCHES.

Soon after this, two laws were promulgated about the same time, one of which was intended to restrain the idolatrous abominations which in time past had been practiced in every city and country, and it provided that no one should erect images, or practice divination and other false and foolish arts, or offer sacrifice in any way.[15] The other statute commanded the erection of oratories on a loftier scale, and the enlargement of the churches of God, as though the hope were entertained that, now the madness of polytheism was wholly removed, almost all mankind would henceforth attach themselves to the service of God. His own personal piety induced the emperor to devise and address these instructions to the governors of the several provinces: and the law further admonished them not to spare the expenditure of money, but to draw supplies from the imperial treasury itself. Similar instructions were written also to the bishops of the several churches; and the emperor was pleased to transmit the same to myself, being the first letter which he personally addressed to me.

CHAPTER XXVIII

CONSTANTINE'S LETTER TO EUSEBIUS AND THE OTHER BISHOPS, RESPECTING THE BUILDING OF CHURCHES, WITH INSTRUCTIONS TO REPAIR THE OLD, AND ERECT NEW ONES ON A LARGER SCALE, WITH THE AID OF THE PROVINCIAL GOVERNORS.

Victor Constantinus, Maximus Augustus, to Eusebius.

Forasmuch as the unholy and willful rule of tyranny has persecuted the servants of our Savior until this present time, I believe and am fully persuaded, best beloved brother, that the buildings belonging to all the churches have either become ruinous through actual neglect, or have received inadequate attention from the dread of the violent spirit of the times.

But now, that liberty is restored, and that serpent[16] driven from the administration of public affairs by the providence of the Supreme God, and our instrumentality, we trust that all can see the efficacy of the Divine power, and that they who through fear of persecution or through unbelief have fallen into any errors, will now acknowledge the true God, and adopt in future that course of life which is according to truth and rectitude. With respect, therefore, to the churches over which you yourself preside, as well as the bishops, presbyters, and deacons of other churches with whom you are acquainted, do you admonish all to be zealous in their attention to the buildings of the churches, and either to repair or enlarge those which at present exist, or, in cases of necessity, to erect new ones.

We also empower you, and the others through you, to demand what is needful for the work, both from the provincial governors and from the Prætorian Prefect. For they have received instructions to be most diligent in obedience to your Holiness's orders.

A copy of this charge was transmitted throughout all the provinces to the bishops of the several churches. The provincial governors received directions accordingly, and the imperial statute was speedily carried into effect.

CHAPTER XXIX

THE EMPEROR WROTE A LETTER ALSO IN CONDEMNATION OF IDOLATRY.

Moreover the emperor, who continually made further progress in piety towards God, despatched an admonitory letter to the inhabitants of every province, respecting the error of idolatry into which his predecessors in power had fallen, in which he eloquently exhorts his subjects to acknowledge the Supreme God, and openly to profess their allegiance to His Christ as their Savior. This letter also I have judged it necessary to translate from the Latin in his own handwriting into the present work, in order that we may hear, as it were, the voice of the emperor himself uttering the following sentiments in the audience of all mankind.

CHAPTER XXX

CONSTANTINE'S EDICT TO THE PEOPLE OF THE PROVINCES CONCERNING THE ERROR OF POLYTHEISM, COMMENCING WITH SOME GENERAL REMARKS ON VIRTUE AND VICE.

Victor Constantinus, Maximus Augustus, to the people of the Eastern provinces.

Whatever is comprehended under the sovereign laws of nature, is capable of conveying to all men an adequate idea of the forethought and intelligence which characterize the arrangements of God. Nor can any, whose minds are directed in the true path of knowledge to the attainment of that end, entertain a doubt that the just perceptions of sound reason, as well as those of the natural vision itself (the true perfection of each faculty having one and the same tendency), lead to the knowledge of God. Accordingly no wise man will ever be surprised when he sees the mass of mankind carried away by pursuits of an entirely opposite character. For the beauty of virtue would be useless and unperceived, did not vice display in contrast with it the course of perversity and folly. Hence it is that the one is crowned with reward, while the most high God is Himself the administrator of judgment to the other.

And now I will endeavor to lay before you all, as explicitly as possible, the nature of my own hopes of future happiness.[17]

The former emperors I have been accustomed to regard as those with whom I could have no sympathy, on account of the savage cruelty of their character. Indeed, my father was the only one who uniformly practiced the duties of humanity, and with admirable piety called for the blessing of God the Father on all his actions. For the rest, following the dictates of a perverted reason, they were more zealous of cruel than gentle measures, and this disposition they indulged without restraint, and thus marred the course of the true doctrine during the whole period of their reign. Nay, so violent did their malicious fury become, that in the midst of a profound peace, as regards both the religious and ordinary interests of men, they kindled as it were the flames of a civil war.[18]

About that time it is said that Apollo spoke from a deep and gloomy cavern, and with no human voice, and declared that the righteous men on earth were a bar to his speaking the truth, and accordingly that the oracles from the tripod were fallacious. Hence it was that he suffered his tresses to droop in token of grief, and mourned the evils which the loss of the oracular spirit would entail on mankind. But let us mark the consequences of this.

I call now on Thee, most high God, to witness that, when very young, I heard him who at that time was chief of the sovereign rulers of the Roman empire (unhappy, truly unhappy as he was, and laboring under deep delusion of soul), make earnest inquiry of his attendants respecting these righteous ones on earth, and that one of the Pagan priests then present replied that they were the Christians. This answer he eagerly received, like some honied draught, and resolved to unsheathe the sword which was ordained for the punishment of crime, against those whose holiness was beyond reproach. Immediately, therefore, he issued those sanguinary edicts, traced, if I may so express myself, with a sword's point dipped in blood, at the same time commanding his judges to tax their ingenuity for the invention of new and more terrible punishments.

Then indeed one might see with what perfect impunity those venerable worshippers of God were daily exposed, with continued and relentless cruelty, to outrages of the most grievous kind, and how that modesty of character which no enemy had ever treated with disrespect, became the mere sport of their infuriated fellow-citizens. Is there any punishment by fire, are there any instruments or modes of torture, which were not applied to all, without distinction of age or sex? Then, it may be truly said, the earth shed tears, the all-encircling compass of heaven mourned because of the pollution of blood, and the very light of day itself was darkened, as it were, in grief and wonder at these scenes of horror.

But is this all? Nay, the barbarians themselves may boast even now of the contrast their conduct presents to these cruel deeds. For they received and kept in gentlest captivity those who then fled from amongst us, and secured to them not merely safety from danger, but also the free exercise of their holy religion. And even now that lasting stain remains, which the flight of the Christians, at that time driven from the Roman world, and their reception by the barbarians, have branded on the Roman name.

But why need I longer dwell on these

lamentable events, and the general sorrow which in consequence pervaded the world? The perpetrators of this dreadful guilt are now no more. They have experienced a miserable end, and are consigned to unceasing punishment in the depths of the lower world. They encountered each other in the fatal arena of civil strife, and have left neither name nor race behind. And surely this calamity would never have befallen them, had not those impious words of the Pythian oracle exercised a delusive power and influence over their minds.

And now I beseech Thee, most mighty God: to be merciful and gracious to Thine Eastern nations, to Thy people in these provinces, bowed and broken as they are by protracted miseries, and vouchsafe them a remedy through Thy servant. Not without cause, O holy God, do I prefer this prayer to Thee, the Lord of all. Under Thy guidance have I devised and accomplished measures fraught with blessing. Preceded by Thy sacred sign I have led Thy armies to victory, and still, on each occasion of public danger, I follow the same symbol of Thy perfections while advancing to meet the foe. Therefore have I dedicated to Thy service a soul duly attempered by love and fear. For Thy name I truly love, while I regard with reverence that power of which Thou hast given abundant proofs, to the confirmation and increase of my faith. I hasten then to devote all my powers to the restoration of that Church which is Thy most holy dwelling-place, and which those profane and impious men have marred by the rude and destroying hand of violence.

My own desire is, for the general advantage of the world and all mankind, that Thy people should enjoy a life of peace and undisturbed concord. Let those, therefore, who are still blinded by error, be made welcome to the same degree of peace and tranquility which they have who believe. For it may be that this restoration of equal privileges to all will have a powerful effect in leading them into the path of truth. Let no one molest another in this matter but let every one be free to follow the bias of his own mind. Only let men of sound judgment be assured of this, that those only can live a life of holiness and purity, whom Thou callest to an acquiescence in Thy holy laws. With regard to those who will hold themselves aloof from us, let them have, if they please, their temples of lies—we have the glorious edifice of Thy truth, which Thou hast given us as our native home.[19] We pray, however, that they too may receive the same blessing, and thus experience that heartfelt joy which unity of sentiment inspires.

And truly our worship is one of no novel or recent character, but such as Thou hast ordained in connexion with the honor due to Thyself from the time when, as we believe, this fair system of the universe was first fitly framed. And, although mankind have deeply fallen, and have been seduced by manifold errors, yet hast Thou revealed a pure light in the person of Thy Son (lest the power of evil should utterly prevail), and hast thus given testimony to all men concerning Thyself.

The truth of this is assured to us by Thy works. It is Thy power which removes our guilt, and makes us faithful. The sun and the moon have their settled course. The stars move in no uncertain orbits round this terrestrial globe. The revolution of the seasons recurs according to unerring laws. The solid fabric of the earth was established by Thy word—the winds receive their impulse at appointed time, and the course of the waters continues with ceaseless flow. The ocean is circumscribed by an immovable barrier. In fine, whatever is comprehended within the compass of the earth and sea is all contrived for wondrous and important ends.

Were it not so, were not all regulated by the determination of Thy will, so great as diversity, so manifold a division of power, would doubtless have brought ruin on the whole course of this world's affairs. Or those agencies which have maintained a mutual strife,[20] would thus have carried to a more deadly length that hostility against the human race which they even now exercise, thought unseen by mortal eyes.

Abundant thanks, most mighty God, and Lord of all, be rendered to Thee on this behalf, that, the better knowledge of our nature is obtained from the diversified pursuits of man, the more are the precepts of Thy divine doctrine confirmed to those whose thoughts are directed aright, and who are sincerely devoted to true virtue. As for those who will not allow themselves to be cured of their error, let them not attribute this to any but themselves. For that remedy which is of sovereign and healing virtue is openly placed within the reach of all. Only let all beware lest they inflict an injury on that religion which experience itself testifies to be pure and undefiled. Henceforward, therefore, let us all enjoy in common the privilege placed within our reach, I mean the blessing of peace. And let us endeavor to keep our conscience pure from aught that might interrupt and mar this blessing.

Once more, let none use that to the detriment of another which he may himself have received on conviction of its truth, but let every one, if it be possible, apply what he has understood and known to the benefit of his neighbor; if otherwise, let him relinquish the attempt. For it is one thing voluntarily to undertake the conflict for immortality, another to compel others to do so from the fear of punishment.

These are our words; and we have enlarged on these topics more than our ordinary clemency would have dictated, because we were unwilling to dissemble or be false to the true faith. And the more so, since we understand there are some who say that the rites of the heathen temples, and the power of darkness, have been entirely removed. We should indeed have earnestly recommended such removal to all men, were it not that the rebellious spirit of those wicked errors still continues obstinately fixed in the minds of some, so as to discourage the hope of any general restoration of mankind to the ways of truth.

CHAPTER XXXI

HOW CONTROVERSIES ORIGINATED AT ALEXANDRIA IN CONNECTION WITH ARIUS.

In this manner the emperor, like a powerful herald of God, addressed himself by his own letter to all the provinces, at the same time warning his subjects against the superstitious errors of idolatry, and encouraging them in the pursuit of true godliness. But in the midst of his joyful anticipations of the success of this measure, he received tidings of a most serious disturbance which had invaded the peace of the Church. This intelligence he heard with deep concern, and at once endeavored to devise a remedy for the evil.

The origin of this disturbance may be thus described. The people of God were in a truly flourishing state, and abounding in the practice of good works. No terror from without assailed them, but a bright and most profound peace, through the favor of God, encompassed His Church on every side. Meantime, however, the spirit of envy was watching to destroy our blessings, which at first crept in unperceived, but soon revelled without restraint in the midst of the assemblies of the saints. At length the same spirit reached the bishops themselves, and arrayed them in angry hostility against each other, on pretence of a jealous regard for the doctrines of Divine truth. Hence it was that a mighty fire was kindled as it were from a little spark, and which, originating in the first instance in the Alexandrian church, overspread the whole of Egypt and Libya, and the further Thebaid. Eventually it extended its ravages to the other provinces and cities of the empire, so that not only the prelates of the churches might be seen encountering each other in the strife of words, but the people themselves were completely divided, and embraced the tenets of opposing parties. Nay, so notorious did the scandal of these proceedings become, that the venerable mysteries of Divine revelation were exposed to the foulest insult and derision in the very theaters of the unbelievers.

CHAPTER XXXII

CONCERNING THE SAME ARIUS, AND THE MELITIANS.[21]

Thus did the adverse parties at Alexandria maintain an obstinate conflict respecting questions of the highest and most mysterious kind. And at the same time others were at variance throughout Egypt and the Upper Thebaid, on account of a controversy which had been still earlier in existence, so that the churches were every where distracted by divisions. The body therefore being thus diseased, the whole of Libya caught the contagion, and the rest of the remoter provinces became affected with the same disorder. For the disputants at Alexandria sent emissaries to the bishops of the several provinces, who accordingly ranged themselves as partisans on either side, and shared in the same spirit of discord.

CHAPTER XXXIII

THAT CONSTANTINE SENT A LETTER, WITH A VIEW TO THE RE-ESTABLISHMENT OF CONCORD.

As soon as the emperor was informed of these facts (which he heard with much sorrow of heart, and considered them in the light of a calamity personally affecting himself), he forthwith selected from the Christians in his train one whom he well knew to be approved for the sobriety and genuineness of his faith,[22] and who had before this time distinguished himself by the boldness of his religious profession, and sent him to act as mediator between the dissentient parties at Alexandria. He also made him the bearer of a most needful and appropriate letter to the original movers of the strife. And this letter, as exhibiting a specimen of his watchful care over God's people, it may be well to introduce into this our narrative of his life. Its purport was as follows.

CHAPTER XXXIV

CONSTANTINE'S LETTER TO ALEXANDER THE BISHOP, AND ARIUS THE PRESBYTER.

Victor Constantinus, Maximus Augustus to Alexander and Arius.

I call that God to witness (as well I may), who

is the helper of my endeavors, and the Preserver of all men, that I had a two-fold reason for undertaking that duty which I have now effectually performed.

My design then was, first, to bring the diverse judgments formed by all nations respecting the Deity to a condition, as it were, of settled uniformity, and secondly, to restore a healthy tone to the system of the world, then suffering under the malignant power of a grievous distemper. Keeping these objects in view, I looked forward to the accomplishment of the one with the secret gaze of the mental eye, while the other I endeavored to secure by the aid of military power. For I was aware that, if I should succeed in establishing, according to my hopes, a common harmony of sentiment among all the servants of God, the general course of affairs would also experience a change correspondent to the pious desires of them all.

Finding, then, that the whole of Africa was pervaded by an intolerable spirit of madness and folly, through the influence of those whose wanton temerity had presumed to rend the religion of the people into diverse sects, I was anxious to allay the virulence of this disorder, and could discover no other remedy equal to the occasion, except in sending some of yourselves to aid in restoring mutual harmony among the disputants, after I had removed that common enemy[23] of mankind who had interposed his lawless sentence for the prohibition of your holy synods.

For since the power of Divine light, and the rule of our holy religion, which have illumined the world by their sacred radiance, proceeded in the first instance, through the favor of God, from the bosom, as it were, of the East, I naturally believed that you would be the first to promote the salvation of other nations, and resolved with all energy of purpose and diligence of inquiry to seek your aid. As soon therefore as I had secured my decisive victory and unquestionable triumph over my enemies, my first inquiry was concerning that object which I felt to be of paramount interest and importance.

But, O glorious Providence of God! How deep a wound did not my ears only, but my very heart receive in the report that, divisions existed among yourselves more grievous still than those which continued in that country![24] So that you, through whose aid I had hoped to procure a remedy for the errors of others, are in a state which demands even more attention than theirs. And yet, having made a careful inquiry into the origin and foundation of these differences, I find the cause to be of a truly insignificant character, and quite unworthy of such fierce contention. Feeling myself, therefore, compelled to address you in this letter, and to appeal at the same time to your unanimity and sagacity, I call on Divine Providence to assist me in the task, while I interrupt your dissension in the character of a minister of peace. And with reason: for if I might expect (with the help of a higher Power) to be able without difficulty, by a judicious appeal to the pious feelings of those who heard me, to recall them to a better spirit, how can I refrain from promising myself a far easier and more speedy adjustment of this difference, when the cause which hinders general harmony of sentiment is intrinsically trifling and of little moment?

I understand, then, that the occasion of your

present controversy is to be traced to the following circumstances: that you, Alexander, demanded of the presbyters what opinion they severally maintained respecting a certain passage in the Divine law,[25] or rather, I should say, that you asked them something connected with an unprofitable question. And then that you, Arius, inconsiderately gave utterance to objections which ought never to have been conceived at all, or if conceived, should have been buried in profound silence. Hence it was that a dissension arose between you, the meeting of the synod was prohibited, and the holy people, rent into diverse parties, no longer preserved the unity of the one body.

Now therefore do ye both exhibit an equal degree of forbearance, and receive the advice which your fellow-servant feels himself justly entitled to give. What then is this advice? It was wrong in the first instance to propose such questions as these, or to reply to them when propounded. For those points of discussion which are enjoined by the authority of no law, but rather suggested by the contentious spirit which is fostered by misused leisure, even though they may be intended merely as an intellectual exercise, ought certainly to be confined to the region of our own thoughts, and neither hastily produced in the public assemblies of the saints, nor unadvisedly intrusted to the general ear. For how very few are there able either accurately to comprehend, or adequately to explain subjects so sublime and abstruse in their nature? Or, granting that one were fully competent for this, in how few ordinary minds will he succeed in producing conviction? Or who, again, in dealing

92

with questions of such subtle nicety as these, can secure himself against a dangerous declension from the truth? It is incumbent therefore on us in these cases to be sparing of our words, lest, in case we ourselves are unable, through the feebleness of our natural faculties, to give a clear explanation of the subject before us, or, on the other hand, in case the slowness of our hearers' understandings disables them from arriving at an accurate apprehension of what we say, from one or other of these causes we reduce the people to the alternative either of blasphemy or schism.

Let therefore both the unguarded question and the inconsiderate answer receive your mutual forgiveness. For your difference has not arisen on any leading doctrines or precepts of the Divine law, nor have you introduced any new dogma respecting the worship of God. You are in truth of one and the same judgment—you may therefore well join in that communion which is the symbol of united fellowship.[26]

For as long as you continue to contend about these truly insignificant questions, it is not fitting that so large a portion of God's people should be under the direction of your judgment, since you are thus divided between yourselves. I believe it indeed to be not merely unbecoming, but positively evil, that such should be the case. But I will appeal to your good sense by a familiar instance to illustrate my meaning. You know that philosophers, while they all adhere to the general tenets of their respective sects, are frequently at issue on some particular assertion or statement. And yet, though they may differ as to the perfection of a principle, they are recalled to harmony of sentiment by the uniting power of their common doctrines. If this be true, is it not far more reasonable that you, who are the ministers of the Supreme God, should be of one mind respecting the profession of the same religion? But let us still more thoughtfully and with closer attention examine what I have said, and see whether it be right that, on the ground of some trifling and foolish verbal difference between ourselves, brethren should assume towards each other the attitude of enemies, and the august meeting of the synod be rent by profane disunion, because we will wrangle together on points so trivial and altogether unessential? Surely this conduct is unworthy of us, and rather characteristic of childish ignorance, than consistent with the wisdom of priests and men of sense. Let us withdraw ourselves with a good will from these temptations of the devil. Our great God and common Savior has granted the same light to us all. Permit me, who am His servant, to bring my task to a successful issue, under the direction of His Providence, that I may be enabled through my exhortations, and diligence, and earnest admonition, to recall His people to the fellowship of one communion. For since you have, as I said, but one faith, and one sentiment respecting our religion, and since the Divine commandment in all its parts enjoins on us all the duty of maintaining a spirit of concord, let not the circumstance which has led to a slight difference between you, since it affects not the general principles of truth, be allowed to prolong any division or schism among you.

And this I say without in any way desiring to force you to entire unity of judgment in regard to this truly idle question, whatever its real nature may be. For the dignity of your synod may be preserved, and the communion of your whole body maintained unbroken, however wide a difference may exist among you as to unimportant matters. For we are not all of us like-minded on every subject, nor is there such a thing as one disposition and judgment common to all alike. As far then as regards the Divine Providence, let there be one faith, and one understanding among you, one united judgment in reference to God. But as to your subtle disputations on questions of little or no significance, though you may be unable to harmonize in sentiment, such differences should be consigned to the secret custody of your own minds and thoughts. And now, let the precious bonds of common affection, let faith in the truth, let the honor due to God and the observance of His law continue immovably established among you. Resume, then, your mutual feelings of affection and regard, permit the whole body of the people once more to unite in that embrace which should be natural to all, and do ye yourselves, having purified your souls, as it were, from every angry thought, once more return to your former fellowship. For it often happens that when a reconciliation is effected by the removal of the causes of enmity, friendship becomes even sweeter than it was before.

Restore me then my quiet days, and untroubled nights, that henceforth the joy of light undimmed by sorrow, the delight of a tranquil life, may continue to be my portion. Else must I needs mourn, with copious and constant tears, nor shall I be able to pass the residue of my days without disquietude. For while the people of God, whose fellow-servant

I am, are thus divided amongst themselves by an unreasonable and pernicious spirit of contention, how is it possible that I shall be able to maintain tranquility of mind? And I will give you a proof how great my sorrow has been on this behalf. Not long since I had visited Nicomedia, and intended forthwith to proceed from that city to the East. It was while I was on the point of hastening towards you, and was already among you in thought and desire, that the news of this matter arrested my intended progress, that I might not be compelled to witness that which I felt myself scarcely able even to hear. Open then for me henceforward by your unity of judgment that road to the regions of the East which your dissensions have closed against me, and permit me speedily to see the happiness both of yourselves and of all other provinces, and to render due acknowledgment to God in the language of praise and thanksgiving for the restoration of general concord and liberty to all.

CHAPTER XXXV

THE CONTROVERSY CONTINUES WITHOUT ABATEMENT, EVEN AFTER THE RECEIPT OF THIS LETTER.

In this manner the pious emperor endeavored by means of the foregoing letter to promote the peace of the Church of God. And the excellent man[27] to whom it was intrusted performed his part not merely by communicating the letter itself, but also by seconding the views of him who sent it. For he was (as I have said) in all respects a person of pious character.

The evil, however, was greater than could be remedied by a single letter, insomuch that the acrimony of the contending parties continually increased, and the effects of the mischief extended to all the Eastern provinces. Such were the fruits of the jealousy of that evil spirit who looked with an envious eye on the prosperity of the Church.

NOTES

1. The reading in the text is τούτων, but should be πάντων, of all Christians, as it is in *History of the Church*, lib. x. c. 8, from which this passage is almost verbally taken.

2. Licinius was suspected of having secretly countenanced Bassianus (who had married Constantine's sister Anastasia, and received the rank of Cæsar), in a treasonable conspiracy. See Gibbon, *Decline and Fall*, chap. xiv. *Note to the 2009 edition:* Not surprisingly, Zosimus puts the full blame for the rupture on Constantine. See *New History*, p. 44.

3. Πάλιν, again, alluding to the former miracle, the vision of the Cross, which Eusebius does not venture to attest himself, but relates on the word and oath of Constantine. See Book I, Chapter XXVIII, p. 23 and Chapter XXX, p. 24.

4. *Note to the 2009 edition*: Zosimus offers a much fuller and more detailed account of the battles between the armies of Constantine and Licinius and holds that they were considerably more evenly contested than Eusebius indicates here. See *New History*, pp. 45–46.

5. This tabernacle, which Constantine always carried with him in his military expeditions, is described by Sozomen, lib. 1. chap. 8; see *Ecclesiastical History*, pp. 21–22.

6. Alluding to Exodus 33:7, etc.

7. "He consented to leave his rival, or, as he again styled Licinius, his friend and brother, in the possession of Thrace, Asia Minor, Syria, and Egypt; but the provinces of Pannonia, Dalmatia, Dacia, Macedonia, and Greece, were yielded to the western empire, and the dominions of Constantine now extended from the confines of Caledonia to the extremity of Peloponnesus." —Gibbon, *Decline and Fall*, chap. xiv.

8. Gibbon (chap. xiv.) says that the reconciliation of Constantine and Licinius maintained, above eight years, the tranquillity of the Roman world. If this be true, it may be regarded as one proof that our author's work is rather to be considered as a general sketch of Constantine's life and character than as a minutely correct historical document.

9. In the gynæcia (γυναικεῖα), or places where women, and

subsequently slaves of both sexes, were employed in spinning and weaving for the emperor. See p. 72 of the present volume.

10. *Note to the 2009 edition:* In the 1845 edition, this excerpt from an original Constantinian document was broken up into several chapters complete with headers added at an early date, but probably not by Eusebius himself (Cameron, p. 54). As these breaks seem superfluous within the body of Constantine's edict, they have been removed in the present edition so that the document might appear as a more coherent whole. Subsequent Constantinian documents appearing here have been treated in the same way.

11. That is, the free subject of inferior rank, accustomed to labor for his subsistence, but not to the degradation of slavery.

12. This seems to be the subscription or signature in the emperor's own hand-writing, which is referred to at the end of Chapter XXIII of the present volume, p. 66.

13. That is, the pro-consuls, the vicars (or vice-prefects), and counts or provincial generals.

14. The power of the four Prætorian Prefects in the time of Constantine is thus described by Gibbon: "1. The Prefect of the East stretched his ample jurisdiction into the three parts of the globe which were subject to the Romans, from the cataracts of the Nile to the banks of the Phasis, and from the mountains of Thrace to the frontiers of Persia. 2. The important provinces of Pannonia, Dacia, Macedonia, and Greece, once acknowledged the authority of the Prefect of Illyricum. 3. The power of the Prefect of Italy was not confined to the country from whence he derived his title; it extended over the additional territory of Rhætia as far as the banks of the Danube, over the dependent islands of the Mediterranean, and over that part of the continent of Africa which lies between the confines of Cyrene and those of Tingitania. 4. The Prefect of the Gauls comprehended under that plural denomination the kindred provinces of Britain and Spain, and his authority was obeyed from the wall of Antoninus to the fort of Mount Atlas." *Decline and Fall*, chap. xvii.

15. That is, private sacrifices: for it appears that the idolatrous temples were allowed to be open for public worship.

16. Licinius, thus designated for the subtlety of his character.

17. The remark of Valesius in reference to the difficulty of this chapter appears probable, viz., that it is partly to be attributed to Constantine's own want of clearness, and partly to his translator, who has rendered obscure Latin into still more obscure Greek.

18. The persecution of the Christians with its attendant horrors, being the act, not of foreign enemies, but of their countrymen and fellow-citizens.

19. Ὅνπερ κατὰ φύσιν δέδωκας. The clause is thus rendered by Valesius: "Nos splendidissimam domum veritatis tuæ, quam nascentibus nobis donasti, retinemus." This seems almost as unintelligible as the original. The translation above attempted yields, perhaps, a sense not inconsistent with the general scope of the passage.

20. Constantine seems here to allude to the gentile deities as powers of evil, capable, if unrestrained by a superior power, of working universal ruin.

21. The Melitians, or Meletians, an obscure Egyptian sect, of whom little satisfactory is recorded.

22. Hosius, bishop of Cordova.

23. Licinius, whose prohibition of synods is referred to in Book I, Chapter LI of the present volume, p. 39. The disputes here mentioned are those between the Catholics and the Donatists, a very violent sect which sprung up in Africa after the persecution by Diocletian.

24. Africa, alluding to the schism of the Donatists.

25. The word νόμος seems to be commonly used by Eusebius as a general term for Divine revelation, as we employ the word "Scripture."

26. The emperor seems at this time to have had a very imperfect knowledge of the errors of the Arian heresy. After the Council of Nicaea, at which he heard them fully explained, he wrote of them in terms of decisive condemnation in his letter to the Alexandrian church. See Socrates *Ecclesiastical History*, p. 30.

27. Hosius of Cordova, mentioned above. See note 22.

BOOK III

CHAPTER I

A COMPARISON OF CONSTANTINE'S PIETY WITH THE WICKEDNESS OF THE PERSECUTORS.

In this manner that Spirit who is the hater of good, actuated by envy at the blessing enjoyed by the Church, continued to raise against her the stormy troubles of intestine discord, in the midst of a period of peace and joy. Meanwhile, however, the divinely favored emperor engaged in no careless spirit in the duties which became his station, but exhibited in his whole conduct a direct contrast to those atrocities of which the cruel tyrants had been lately guilty, and thus triumphed over every enemy that opposed him.

For in the first place, the tyrants, being themselves alienated from the true God, had enforced by every compulsion the worship of false deities: Constantine convinced mankind by actions as well as words, that these had but an imaginary existence, and exhorted them to acknowledge the only true God.

They had derided His Christ with words of blasphemy: he assumed that as his safeguard against which they launched their impious invectives, and gloried in the symbol of the Savior's passion.

They had persecuted and driven into houseless exile the servants of Christ: he recalled them every one, and restored them to their native homes.

They had covered them with dishonor: he made their condition honorable and enviable in the eyes of all.

The tyrants had shamefully plundered and sold the goods of godly men: Constantine not only replaced this loss, but still further enriched them with abundant presents.

They had circulated injurious calumnies, through their written ordinances, against the prelates of the Church: he, on the contrary, conferred dignity on these individuals by personal marks of honor, and by his edicts and statutes raised them to higher distinction than before.

They had utterly demolished and razed to the ground the houses of prayer: he commanded that those which still existed should be enlarged, and that new ones should be raised on a magnificent scale at the expense of the imperial treasury.

They had ordered the inspired records to be burnt and destroyed: he decreed that copies of them should be multiplied, and magnificently adorned at the charge of the imperial treasury.

They had strictly forbidden the prelates, anywhere or on any occasion, to convene synods; whereas he gathered them to his court from every province, invited them to his palace, gave them constant access to his person, and admitted them to a share of his imperial hospitality.

The tyrants had honored the demons with offerings: Constantine exposed their frauds, and continually distributed the now useless materials for sacrifice, to those who would apply them to a better use.

They had ordered the pagan temples to be sumptuously adorned: he razed to their foundations those of them which had been the chief objects of superstitious reverence.

They had subjected God's servants to the most ignominious punishments: he took vengeance on the persecutors, and inflicted on them just chastisement in the name of God, while he held the memory of His holy martyrs in constant veneration.

They had driven God's worshippers from the imperial palaces: he placed full confidence in them at all times, and esteemed them more zealous and faithful than any beside.

They, the victims of avarice, voluntarily subjected themselves as it were to the pangs of Tantalus: he with royal magnificence unlocked all his treasures, and distributed his gifts with rich and high-souled liberality.

The tyrants had been stained with the guilt of countless murders, that they might plunder or confiscate the wealth of their victims: while throughout the reign of Constantine the sword of justice hung idle everywhere, and both people and municipal magistrates[1] in every province, were rather constrained by a paternal authority than governed by the stringent power of the laws.

Surely it must seem to all who duly regard these facts, that a new and fresh era of existence had begun to appear, and a light heretofore unknown suddenly to dawn from the midst of darkness on the human race. And all must confess that these things were entirely the work of God, who raised up this pious emperor to withstand the multitude of the ungodly.

CHAPTER II

FURTHER REMARKS ON CONSTANTINE'S PIETY, AND HIS OPEN PROFESSION OF THE CROSS.

And when we consider that their iniquities were without example, and the atrocities which they dared to perpetrate against the Church such as had never been heard of in any age of the world, well might God Himself bring before us something entirely new, and work thereby effects such as had hitherto been never either recorded or observed. And what miracle was ever more marvellous than the virtues of this our emperor, whom the wisdom of God has vouchsafed as a gift to the human race? For truly he maintained a continual testimony to His Christ with all boldness and before all men. And so far was he from shrinking from an open profession of the Christian name, that he rather desired to make it manifest to all that he regarded this as his highest honor, whether it were by impressing on his face the salutary sign, or glorying in it as the trophy which led him on to victory.

CHAPTER III

OF HIS PICTURE SURMOUNTED BY A CROSS, AND HAVING BENEATH IT A WOUNDED DRAGON

And beside this, he caused to be painted on a lofty tablet, and set up in the front of the portico of his palace, so as to be visible to all, a representation of the salutary sign placed above his head, and below it that hateful savage adversary of mankind, who by means of the tyranny of the ungodly had wasted the Church of God falling headlong, under the form of a dragon, to the abyss of destruction. For the sacred oracles in the books of God's prophets have described him as a dragon and a crooked serpent; and for this reason the emperor thus publicly displayed a painted[2] resemblance of the dragon beneath his own and his children's feet, stricken through with a dart, and cast headlong into the sea.

In this manner he intended to represent the secret adversary of the human race, and to indicate that he was consigned to the gulf of perdition by virtue of the salutary trophy placed above his head. This allegory, then, was thus conveyed by means of the colors of a picture. And I am filled with wonder at what I may call the divine sagacity of the emperor, who thus vividly expressed what the prophets had foretold concerning this monster: that God would bring His great and strong and terrible sword against the dragon, the flying serpent, and would destroy the dragon that was in the sea. This it was of which the emperor gave a true and faithful representation in the picture above described.

CHAPTER IV

A FURTHER NOTICE OF THE CONTROVERSIES RAISED IN EGYPT THROUGH THE INSTRUMENTALITY OF ARIUS.

In such occupations as these he employed himself with pleasure. But the effects of that envious spirit which so disturbed the peace of the Churches of God in Alexandria, together with the Theban and Egyptian schism, continued to cause him no little anxiety of mind. For in fact, in every city bishops were engaged in obstinate conflict with bishops, and people rising against people, and almost, like the fabled Symplegades, coming into violent collision with each other.[3] Nay, some were so far transported beyond the bounds of reason as to be guilty of reckless and outrageous conduct, and even to insult the statues of the emperor. This state of things had little power to excite his anger, but rather caused in him sorrow of spirit, for he deeply deplored the folly thus exhibited by misguided men.

CHAPTER V

OF THE DISSENSIONS RESPECTING THE CELEBRATION OF EASTER.

But before this time another most virulent disorder had existed, and long afflicted the Church—I mean the difference respecting the salutary feast of Easter. For while one party asserted that the Jewish custom should be adhered to, the other affirmed that the exact recurrence of the period should be observed, without following the authority of those who were in error, and strangers to the grace of the gospel as well in this as in other respects.

Accordingly, the people being thus in every place divided, and the sacred observances of religion confounded for a long period (insomuch that the diversity of judgment in regard to the time for celebrating one and the same feast, caused the bitterest disunion between those who kept it, some afflicting themselves with fastings and austerities, while others devoted their time to festive relaxation), no one appeared who was capable of devising a remedy for the evil, because the controversy continued equally balanced between both parties. To God alone, the Almighty, was the healing of these differences an easy task, and Constantine appeared to be the only one on earth capable of being His minister for this good end. For as soon as he was made acquainted with the facts which I have described, and perceived that his letter to the Alexandrian Christians had failed to produce its due effect, he at once aroused the energies of his mind, and declared that he must prosecute to the utmost this war also against the secret adversary who was disturbing the peace of the Church.

CHAPTER VI

HE ORDERS A COUNCIL TO ASSEMBLE AT NICAEA.

Resolved, therefore, to bring as it were a divine array against this enemy, he convoked a general council, and invited the speedy attendance of bishops from all quarters, in letters expressive of the honorable estimation in which he held them. Nor was this merely the issuing of a bare command, but the emperor's condescension contributed much to its being carried into effect, for he allowed some the use of the public means of conveyance, while he afforded to others an ample supply of horses for their transport. The place, too, selected for the synod, the city Nicaea in Bithynia (which derived its name from Victory), was appropriate to the occasion. As soon then as the imperial injunction was generally made known, all with the utmost celerity hastened to obey it, as though they would outstrip one another in a race, for they were impelled by the anticipation of a happy result to the conference, by the hope of enjoying present peace, and the desire of beholding something new and strange in the person of so admirable an emperor. Now when they were all assembled, it appeared evident that the proceeding was the work of God, inasmuch as men who had been most widely separated, not merely in sentiment, but also personally, and by difference of country, place, and nation, were here brought together, and comprised within the walls of a single city, forming as it were a vast garland of priests, composed of a variety of the choicest flowers.

CHAPTER VII

OF THE GENERAL COUNCIL, AT WHICH BISHOPS FROM ALL NATIONS WERE PRESENT.

In effect, the most distinguished of God's ministers from all the Churches which abounded in Europe, Africa, and Asia, were here assembled. And a single house of prayer, as though divinely enlarged, sufficed to contain at once Syrians and Cilicians, Phœnicians and Arabians, delegates from Palestine, and others from Egypt, Thebans and Libyans, with those who came from the region of Mesopotamia. A Persian bishop too was present at this conference, nor was even a Scythian found wanting to the number. Pontus, Galatia, and Pamphylia, Cappadocia, Asia, and Phrygia, furnished their most distinguished prelates, while those who dwelt in the remotest districts of Thrace and Macedonia, of Achaia and Epirus, were notwithstanding in attendance. Even from Spain itself, one whose fame was widely spread took his seat as an individual in the great assembly,[4] The prelate of the imperial city[5] was prevented from attending by extreme old age, but his presbyters were present, and supplied his place. Constantine is the first prince of any age who bound together such a garland as this with the bond of peace, and presented it to Christ his Savior as a thank-offering for the victories he had obtained over every foe, thus exhibiting in our own times a similitude of the apostolic company.

CHAPTER VIII

THE ASSEMBLY WAS COMPOSED, AS IN THE ACTS OF THE APOSTLES, OF INDIVIDUALS FROM VARIOUS NATIONS.

For it is said that in the Apostles' age, devout men were gathered from every nation under heaven, among whom were Parthians, and Medes, and Elamites, and the dwellers in Mesopotamia, and in Judea, and Cappadocia, in Pontus and Asia, Phrygia and Pamphylia, in Egypt, and the parts of Libya about Cyrene, and strangers of Rome, Jews and proselytes, Cretes and Arabians.[6] Now the defect of that assembly was, that not all who composed it were ministers of God. But in the present company, the number of bishops exceeded two hundred and fifty, while that of the presbyters and deacons in their train, and the crowd of acolytes and other attendants was altogether beyond computation.

CHAPTER IX

OF THE VIRTUE AND AGE OF THE TWO HUNDRED AND FIFTY BISHOPS.

Of these ministers of God, some were distinguished by wisdom and eloquence, others by the gravity of their lives, and by patient fortitude of character, while others again united in themselves all these graces. There were among them men whose years demanded the tribute of respect and veneration. Others were younger and in the prime of bodily an mental vigor, and some had but recently entered on the course of their ministry. For the maintenance of all a sumptuous provision was daily furnished by the emperor's command.

CHAPTER X

MEETING IN THE PALACE AT WHICH CONSTANTINE APPEARED AND TOOK HIS SEAT IN THE ASSEMBLY.

Now when the appointed day arrived on which the council met for the final solution of the questions in dispute, each member attended to deliver his judgement in the central building of the palace,[7] which appeared to exceed the rest in magnitude. On each side of the interior of this were many seats disposed in order, which were occupied by those who had been invited to attend, according to their rank. As soon, then, as the whole assembly had seated themselves with becoming gravity, a general silence prevailed, in expectation of the emperor's arrival. And first of all three of his immediate family entered in succession, and others also preceded his approach, not of the soldiers or guards who usually accompanied him, but only friends who avowed the faith of Christ. And now, all rising at the signal which indicated the emperor's entrance, at last he himself proceeded through the midst of the assembly, like some heavenly messenger of God, clothed in raiment which glittered as it were with rays of light, reflecting the glowing radiance of a purple robe, and adorned with the brilliant splendor of gold and precious stones. Such was the external appearance of his person, and with regard to his mind, it was evident that he was distinguished by piety and godly fear. This was indicated by his downcast eyes, the blush on his countenance, and the modesty of his gait. For the rest of his personal excellencies, he surpassed all present in height of stature and beauty of form, as well as in majestic dignity of mien, and invincible strength and vigor. All these graces, united to a suavity of manner, and a serenity becoming his imperial station, declared the excellence of his mental qualities to be above all praise. As soon as he had advanced to the upper end of the seats, at first he remained standing, and when a low chair of wrought gold had been set for him, he waited until the bishops had beckoned to him, and then sat down, and after him the whole assembly did the same.

CHAPTER XI

SILENCE OF THE COUNCIL, AFTER SOME WORDS SPOKEN BY THE BISHOP EUSEBIUS.

The bishop who occupied the chief place in the right division of the assembly[8] then rose, and, addressing the emperor, delivered a concise speech, in a strain of praise and thanksgiving to Almighty God on his behalf. When he had resumed his seat, silence ensued, and all regarded the emperor with fixed attention, on which he looked serenely round on the assembly with a cheerful aspect, and having collected his thoughts in a gentle tone gave utterance to the following words.

CHAPTER XII

CONSTANTINE'S ADDRESS TO THE COUNCIL,
IN PRAISE OF PEACE.

It was once my chief desire, dearest friends, to enjoy the spectacle of your united presence. And now that this desire is fulfilled, I feel myself bound to render thanks to God the universal King, because in addition to all His other benefits, He has granted me a blessing higher than all the rest, in permitting me to see you not only all assembled together, but all united in a common harmony of sentiment. I pray therefore that no malignant adversary may henceforth interfere to mar our happy state. I pray that now the impious hostility of the tyrants has been forever removed by the power of God our Savior, that spirit who delights in evil may devise no other means for exposing the divine records to blasphemous calumny. For, in my judgment, internal strife within the Church of God is far more evil and dangerous than any kind of war or conflict, and these our differences appear to me more grievous than any outward trouble. Accordingly, when by the will and with the co-operation of God, I had been victorious over my enemies, and thought that nothing more remained but to render thanks to Him, and sympathize in the joy of those whom he had restored to freedom through my instrumentality, as soon as I heard that intelligence which I had least expected to receive—I mean the news of your dissension—I judged it to be of no secondary importance, but with the earnest desire that a remedy for this evil also might be found

111

through my means, immediately sent to require your presence. And now I rejoice in beholding your assembly. But I feel that my desires will be most completely fulfilled when I can see you all united in one judgment, and that common spirit of peace and concord prevailing amongst you all, which it becomes you, as consecrated to the service of God, to commend to others. Delay not, then, dear friends: delay not, ye ministers of God, and faithful servants of Him who is our common Lord and Savior. Begin from this moment to discard the causes of that disunion which has existed among you, and remove the perplexities of controversy by embracing the principles of peace. For by such conduct you will at the same time be acting in a manner most pleasing to God, and you will confer an exceeding favor on me who am your fellow-servant.

CHAPTER XIII

IN WHAT MANNER HE LED THE DISSENTIENT BISHOPS TO UNITE IN HARMONY OF SENTIMENT.

As soon as the emperor had spoken these words in the Latin tongue, which another present rendered into Greek, he gave permission to those who presided in the council to deliver their opinions. On this some began to accuse their neighbors, who defended themselves, and recriminated in their turn. In this numberless assertions were put forth by each party, and a violent controversy arose at the very commencement. Notwithstanding this, the emperor gave patient audience to all alike, and received every proposition with steadfast attention, and by occasionally assisting the argument of each party in turn, he gradually disposed even the most vehement disputants to a reconciliation. At the same time, by the affability of his address to all, and his use of the Greek language (with which he was not altogether unacquainted), he appeared in a truly attractive and amiable light, persuading some, convincing others by his reasonings, praising those who spoke well, and urging all to unity of sentiment, until at last he succeeded in bringing them to one mind and judgment respecting every disputed question.

CHAPTER XIV

UNANIMOUS DECLARATION OF THE COUNCIL CONCERNING FAITH, AND THE CELEBRATION OF EASTER.

The result was that they were not only united as concerning the faith, but that the time for the celebration of the salutary feast of Easter was agreed on by all. Those points also which were sanctioned by the resolution of the whole body were committed to writing, and received the signature of each several member, and then the emperor, believing that he had thus obtained a second victory over the adversary of the Church, proceeded to solemnize a triumphal festival in honor of God.

CHAPTER XV

CONSTANTINE ENTERTAINS THE BISHOPS ON THE OCCASION OF HIS VICENNALIA.

About this time he completed the twentieth year of his reign. On this occasion public festivals were celebrated by the people of the provinces generally, but the emperor himself invited and feasted with those ministers of God whom he had reconciled, and thus offered as it were through them a suitable sacrifice to God. Not one of the bishops was wanting at the imperial banquet, the circumstances of which were splendid beyond description. Detachments of the bodyguard and other troops surrounded the entrance of the palace with drawn swords, and through the midst of these the men of God proceeded without fear into the innermost of the imperial apartments, in which some were the emperor's own companions at table, while others reclined on couches arranged on either side. One might have thought that a picture of Christ's kingdom was thus shadowed forth, and that the scene was less like reality, than a dream.

CHAPTER XVI

PRESENTS TO THE BISHOPS, AND LETTERS ADDRESSED TO THE PEOPLE GENERALLY.

After the celebration of this brilliant festival, the emperor courteously received all his guests, and generously added to the favors he had already bestowed by personally presenting gifts to each individual according to his rank. He also gave information of the proceedings of the synod to those who had not been present, by a letter in his own hand-writing. And this letter also I will inscribe as it were on a tablet by inserting it in this my narrative of his life. It was as follows:—

CHAPTER XVII

CONSTANTINE'S LETTER TO THE CHURCHES RESPECTING THE COUNCIL AT NICAEA.

Constantinus Augustus, to the Churches.

Having had full proof, in the general prosperity of the empire, how great the favor of God has been towards us, I have judged that it ought to be the first object of my endeavors, that unity of faith, sincerity of love, and community of feeling in regard to the worship of Almighty God, might be preserved among the highly favored multitude who compose the Catholic Church. And, inasmuch as this object could not be effectually and certainly secured, unless all, or at least the greater number of the bishops were to meet together, and a discussion of all particulars relating to our most holy religion to take place, for this reason as numerous an assembly as possible has been convened, at which I myself was present, as one among yourselves (and far be it from me to deny that which is my greatest joy, that I am your fellow-servant), and every question received due and full examination, until that judgment which God, who sees all things, could approve, and which tended to unity and concord, was brought to light, so that no room was left for further discussion or controversy in relation to the faith.

At this meeting the question concerning the most holy day of Easter was discussed, and it was resolved by the united judgment of all present, that this feast ought to be kept by all and in every place on one and the same day. For what can be more becoming or honorable to us than that this feast, from which we date our hopes of immortality, should be observed unfailing by all alike, according to one ascertained order and arrangement? And first of all, it appeared an unworthy thing that in the celebration of this most holy feast we should follow the practice of the Jews, who have impiously defiled their hands with enormous sin, and are therefore deservedly afflicted with blindness of soul. For we have it in our power, if we abandon their custom, to prolong the due observance of this ordinance to future ages, by a truer order, which we have preserved from the very day of the passion until the present time. Let us then have nothing in common with the detestable Jewish crowd, for we have received from our Savior a different way. A course at once legitimate and honorable lies open to our most holy religion. Beloved brethren, let us with one consent adopt this course, and withdraw ourselves from all participation in their baseness.[9]

For their boast is absurd indeed, that it is not in our power without instruction from them to observe these things. For how should they be capable of firming a sound judgment, who, since their parricidal guilt in slaying their Lord, have been subject to the direction, not of reason, but of ungoverned passion, and are swayed by every impulse of the mad spirit that is in them? Hence it is that on this point as well as others they have no perception of the truth, so that being altogether ignorant of the true adjustment of this question, they sometimes celebrate Easter twice in the same year. Why then should we follow those who are confessedly in grievous error? Surely we shall never consent to keep this feast a second time in the same year.

But supposing these reasons were not of sufficient weight, still it would be incumbent on your Sagacities[10] to strive and pray continually that the unity of your souls may not seem in anything to be sullied by fellowship with the customs of these most wicked men. We must consider, too, that a discordant judgment in a case of such importance, and respecting such a solemnity of our religion, must needs be contrary to the Divine will. For our Savior has left us one feast in commemoration of the day of our deliverance—I mean the day of

116

His most holy passion—and He has willed that
His Catholic Church should be one, the members
of which, however scattered in many and diverse
places, are yet cherished by one pervading spirit,
that is, by the will of God. And let your Holinesses'
sagacity reflect how grievous and scandalous it is
that on the self-same days some should be engaged
in fasting, others in festive enjoyment, and again,
that after the days of Easter some should lend their
countenance to banquets and amusements, while
others are fulfilling the appointed fasts.

It is, then, plainly the will of Divine Providence
(as I suppose you all clearly see), that this usage
should receive fitting correction, and be reduced to
one uniform rule.

Since, therefore, it was needful that this matter
should be rectified, so that we might have nothing
in common with that nation of parricides who slew
their Lord; and since that arrangement is consistent
with propriety which is observed by all the churches
of the western, southern, and northern parts of the
world, and by some of the eastern also: for these
reasons all are unanimous on this present occasion
in thinking it worthy of adoption. And I myself
have undertaken that this decision should meet
with the approval of your Sagacities, in the hope
that your Wisdoms will gladly admit that practice
which is observed at once in the city of Rome,
and in Africa; throughout Italy, and in Egypt; in
Spain, the Gauls, Britain, Libya, and the whole of
Greece, in the dioceses of Asia and Pontus, and in
Cilicia, with entire unity of judgment. And you will
consider not only that the number of churches is far
greater in the regions I have enumerated than in any

other, but also that it is most fitting that all should unite in desiring that which sound reason appears to demand, and in avoiding all participation in the perjured conduct of the Jews.[11] In fine, that I may express my meaning in as few words as possible, it has been determined by the common judgment of all, that the most holy feast of Easter should be kept on one and the same day. For on the one hand a discrepancy of opinion on so sacred a question is unbecoming, and on the other it is surely best to act on a decision which is free from error.

Receive, then, with all willingness this truly Divine injunction, and regard it as the gift of God. For whatever is determined in the holy assemblies of the bishops is to be regarded as indicative of the Divine will. As soon, therefore, as you have communicated these proceedings to all our beloved brethren, you are bound from that time forward to adopt for yourselves, and to enjoin on others the arrangement above mentioned, and the due observance of this most sacred day, that whenever I come into the presence of your love (which I have long desired), I may have it in my power to celebrate the holy feast with you on the same day, and may rejoice with you on all accounts, when I behold the cruel power of Satan removed by Divine aid through the agency of our endeavors, while your faith, and peace, and concord everywhere flourish.

God preserve you, beloved brethren!

The emperor transmitted a faithful copy of this letter to every province, wherein they who read it might discern as in a mirror the pure sincerity of his thoughts, and of his piety toward God.

CHAPTER XVIII

HE EXHORTS THE BISHOPS, ON THEIR DEPARTURE, TO PRESERVE A SPIRIT OF CONCORD.

And now, when the council was on the point of being finally dissolved, he summoned all the bishops to meet him on an appointed day, and on their arrival addressed them in a farewell speech, in which he recommended them to be diligent in the maintenance of peace, and the avoidance of contentious disputations, amongst themselves. He cautioned them also against a spirit of jealousy, should any one of their number appear pre-eminent for wisdom and eloquence, bidding them esteem the excellence of one a blessing common to all.

On the other hand he reminded them that the more gifted should forbear to exalt themselves to the prejudice of their humbler brethren, since it is God's prerogative to judge of real superiority. Rather should they considerately condescend to the weaker, remembering that absolute perfection in any case is a rare quality indeed. Each, then, should be willing to accord indulgence to the other for slight offences, to forgive and pass over mere human errors, holding mutual harmony in the highest honor, that no occasion of mockery might be given by their dissensions to those who are ever ready to blaspheme the word of God, for whose benefit indeed we should do all in our power, as for those who might be saved, were our State and conduct exhibited before them in an attractive light.

Meantime they should be well aware of the fact, that the testimony given is by no means productive of blessing to all, since some who hear are glad to secure the supply of their mere bodily necessities while others court the patronage of their superiors; some fix their affection on those who treat them with hospitable kindness, others again, being honored with presents, love their benefactors in return. But few are they who really desire the word of testimony, and rare indeed is it to find a friend of truth. Hence the necessity of endeavoring to meet the case of all, and physician-like, to administer to each that which may tend to the health of the soul, to the end that the saving doctrine may be fully honored by all. Of this kind was the former part of his exhortation, and in conclusion he enjoined them to offer diligent supplications to God on his behalf. Having thus taken leave of them, he gave them all permission to return to their respective countries. And this they did with joy, and thenceforward that unity of judgment at which they had arrived in the emperor's presence continued to prevail, and those who had long been divided were bound together as members of the same body.

CHAPTER XIX
HAVING HONORABLY DISMISSED SOME, HE WROTE LETTERS TO OTHERS, BESTOWING LIKEWISE PRESENTS IN MONEY.

Full of joy therefore at this success, the emperor presented as it were fair and pleasant fruits in the way of letters to those who had not been present at the council. He commanded also that ample gifts of money should be bestowed on all the people, both in the country and the cities being pleaded thus to honor the festive occasion of the twentieth anniversary of his reign.

CHAPTER XX
HE WRITES TO THE EGYPTIANS, EXHORTING THEM TO PEACE.

And now, when all else were at peace, among the Egyptians alone an implacable contention still raged, so as once more to disturb the emperor's tranquillity, though not to excite his anger. For indeed he treated the contending parties with all respect, as fathers, nay rather, as prophets of God. And again he summoned them to his presence, and again patiently acted as mediator between them, and honored them with gifts. He communicated also the result of his arbitration by letter, confirming and sanctioning the decrees of the council, and calling on them to strive earnestly for concord, and not to distract and rend the Church, but to keep before them the thought of God's judgment on this behalf. And these injunctions he sent by a letter written with his own hand.

CHAPTER XXI

HE WRITES FREQUENT LETTERS OF A RELIGIOUS CHARACTER TO THE BISHOPS AND PEOPLE.

But besides these, his writings are very numerous on kindred subjects, and he was the author of a multitude of letters, some to the bishops, in which he laid injunctions on them tending to the advantage of the churches of God. And sometimes, thrice blessed as he was, he addressed the people of the churches generally, calling them his own brethren and fellow-servants. But perhaps we may hereafter find leisure to collect these dispatches in a separate form, in order that the integrity of our present history may not be impaired by their insertion.

CHAPTER XXII

HE ORDERS THE ERECTION OF A CHURCH AT JERUSALEM, IN THE HOLY PLACE OF OUR SAVIOR'S RESURRECTION.

After these things, the pious emperor addressed himself to another work truly worthy of record, in the province of

Palestine. What then was this work? He judged it incumbent on him to render the blessed locality of our Savior's resurrection an object of attraction and veneration to all. He issued immediate injunctions, therefore, for the erection in that spot of a house of prayer. And this he did, not on the mere natural impulse of his own mind, but feeling his spirit directed thereto by the Savior Himself.

CHAPTER XXIII

HOW THE HOLY SEPULCHER HAD BEEN COVERED WITH RUBBISH AND PROFANED WITH IDOLS BY THE UNGODLY.

For it had been in time past the endeavor of impious men (or rather let me say of the whole race of evil spirits through their means), to consign to the darkness of oblivion that divine monument, of immortality to which the radiant angel had descended from heaven, and rolled away the stone for those who still had stony hearts, and who supposed that the living One still lay among the dead, and had declared glad tidings to the women also, and removed their stony-hearted unbelief by the conviction that He whom they sought was alive.

This sacred cave, then, certain impious and godless persons had thought to remove entirely from the eyes of men, supposing in their folly that thus they should be able effectually to obscure the truth. Accordingly they brought a quantity of earth from a distance with much labor, and covered the entire spot. Then, having raised this to a moderate height, they paved it with stone, concealing the holy cave beneath this massive mound. Then, as though their purpose had been effectually accomplished, they prepared on this foundation a truly dreadful sepulcher of souls, by building a gloomy shrine of lifeless idols to the impure spirit whom they call Venus, and offering detestable oblations therein on profane and accursed altars. For they supposed that their object could not otherwise be fully attained, than by thus burying the sacred cave beneath these foul pollutions. Unhappy men! They were unable to comprehend how impossible it was that their attempt should remain unknown to Him who had been crowned with victory over death, any more than the blazing sun, when he rises above the earth, and holds his wonted course through the midst of heaven, is unseen by the whole race of mankind. Indeed, His saving power, shining with still greater brightness, and illumining, not the bodies, but the souls of men, was already filling the world with its own light.

Nevertheless, these devices of impious and wicked men against the truth had prevailed for a long time, nor had any one of the governors, or military commanders, or even of the emperors themselves ever yet appeared, with ability to abolish these daring impieties, save only our prince, who enjoyed the favor of the King of kings. And now, acting as he did under the guidance of His Spirit, he could not consent to see the sacred spot of which we have spoken thus buried, through the devices of the adversaries, under every kind of impurity, and abandoned to obscenity and neglect. Nor would he yield to the malice of those who had contracted this guilt, but gave orders that the place should be thoroughly purified, thinking that the parts which had been most polluted by the enemy ought to receive special tokens, through his means, of the greatness of the Divine favor. As soon, then, as his commands were issued, these engines of deceit were cast down from their proud eminence to the very ground, and the dwelling places of error, with the statues and the evil spirits which they represented, were overthrown and utterly destroyed.

CHAPTER XXIV

CONSTANTINE COMMANDS THE MATERIALS OF THE IDOL-TEMPLE, AND THE SOIL ITSELF, TO BE REMOVED AND THROWN TO A DISTANCE.

Nor did the emperor's zeal stop here, but he gave further orders that the materials of what was thus destroyed, both stone and timber, should be removed and thrown as far from the spot as possible. And this command also was speedily executed. The emperor, however, was not satisfied with having proceeded thus far. Once more, fired with holy ardor, he directed that the ground itself should be dug up to a considerable depth, and the soil which had been polluted by the foul impurities of demon worship transported to a far distant place.

CHAPTER XXV

DISCOVERY OF THE MOST HOLY SEPULCHER.

This also was accomplished without delay. But as soon as the original surface of the ground, beneath the covering of earth, appeared, immediately, and contrary to all expectation, the venerable and hallowed monument of our Savior's resurrection was discovered. Then indeed did this most holy cave present a faithful similitude of His return to life, in that, after lying buried in darkness, it again emerged to light, and afforded to all who came to witness the sight, a clear and visible proof of the wonders of which that spot had once been the scene, a testimony to the resurrection of the Savior clearer than any voice could give.

CHAPTER XXVI

HE WRITES CONCERNING THE ERECTION OF A CHURCH, BOTH TO THE GOVERNORS OF THE PROVINCES, AND TO THE BISHOP MACARIUS.

Immediately after the transactions I have recorded, the emperor sent forth injunctions which breathed a truly pious spirit, at the same time granting ample supplies of money, and commanding that a house of prayer worthy of the worship of God should be erected near the Savior's tomb on a scale of rich and royal greatness. This object he had indeed for some time kept in view, and had foreseen, as if by the aid of a superior intelligence, that which should afterwards come to pass. He laid his commands, therefore, on the governors of the Eastern provinces, that by an abundant and unsparing expenditure they should secure the completion of the work on a scale of noble and ample magnificence. He also dispatched the following letter to the bishop who at that time presided over the church at Jerusalem, in which he clearly asserted the saving doctrine of the faith, writing in these terms.

CHAPTER XXVII

CONSTANTINE'S LETTER TO MACARIUS RESPECTING THE BUILDING OF A MEMORIAL OF OUR SAVIOR'S DEATH.

Victor Constantinus Maximus Augustus, to Macarius.

Such is our Savior's grace, that no power of language seems adequate to describe the wondrous circumstance to which I am about to refer. For, that the monument of His most holy Passion, so long ago buried beneath the ground, should have remained unknown for so long a series of years, until its reappearance to His servants now set free through the removal of him[12] who was the common enemy of all, is a fact which truly surpasses all admiration. For if all who are accounted wise throughout the world were to unite in their endeavors to say something worthy of this event, they would be unable to attain their object in the smallest degree. Indeed, the nature of this miracle as far transcends the capacity of human reason as heavenly things are superior to the interests of men. For this cause it is ever my first, and indeed my only object, that as the authority of the truth is evincing itself daily by fresh wonders, so our souls may all become more zealous, with all sobriety and earnest unanimity, for the honor of the Divine law. I desire, therefore, especially, that you should be persuaded of that which I suppose is evident to all beside, namely, that I have no greater care than how I may best adorn with a splendid structure that sacred spot which, under Divine direction, I have disencumbered as it were of the heavy weight of foul idol worship—a spot which has been accounted holy from the beginning in God's judgment, but which now appears holier still, since it has brought to light a clear assurance of our Savior's passion.

It will be well, therefore, for your Sagacity to make such arrangements and provision of all things needful for the work, that not only the church itself as a whole may surpass all others whatsoever in beauty, but that the details of the building may be of such a kind that the fairest structures in any city of the empire may be excelled by this. And with respect to the erection and decoration of the walls, this is to inform you that our friend Dracilianus, the deputy of the Prætorian Prefects, and the governor of the province, have received a charge from us. For our pious directions to them are to the effect that artificers and laborers, and whatever they shall understand from your Sagacity to be needful for the advancement of the work, shall forthwith be furnished by their care. And as to the columns and marbles, whatever you shall judge, after actual inspection of the plan, to be especially precious and serviceable, be diligent to send information to us in writing, in order that whatever materials and in whatever quantity we shall esteem from our letter to be needful, may be procured from every quarter, as required.

With respect to the roof of the church, I wish to know from you whether in your judgment it should be ceiled, or finished with any other kind of workmanship. If the ceiling be adopted, it may also be ornamented with gold. For the rest, your Holiness will give information as early as possible to the before-mentioned magistrates how many laborers and artificers, and what expenditure of money is required. You will also be careful to send us a report without delay, not only respecting the marbles and columns, but the ceiling also, should this appear to you to be the most beautiful form.

God preserve you, beloved brother!

CHAPTER XXVIII

HOW THE CHURCH OF OUR SAVIOR WAS BUILT, WHICH ANSWERED TO THE NEW JERUSALEM PROPHESIED OF IN SCRIPTURE.

This was the emperor's letter, and his directions were at once carried into effect. Accordingly, on the very spot which witnessed the Savior's sufferings, a new Jerusalem was constructed, over against the one so celebrated of old, which, since the foul stain of guilt brought on it by the murder of the Lord, had experienced the last extremity of desolation, the effect of Divine judgment on its impious people. It was opposite this city that the emperor now began to rear a monument to the Savior's victory over death, with rich and lavish magnificence. And it may be that this was that second and new Jerusalem spoken of in the predictions of the prophets,[13] concerning which such abundant testimony is given in the divinely inspired records.

First of all, then, he adorned the sacred cave itself, as the chief part of the whole work, and the hallowed monument at which the angel radiant with light had once declared to all that regeneration which was first manifested in the Savior's person.

CHAPTER XXIX

DESCRIPTION OF THE FABRIC OF THE HOLY SEPULCHER.

This monument, therefore, first of all, as the chief part of the whole, the emperor's zealous magnificence beautified with rare columns, and profusely enriched with the most, splendid decorations of every kind.[14]

The next object of his attention was a space of ground

of great extent, and open to the pure air of heaven. This he adorned with a pavement of finely polished stone, and enclosed it on three sides with porticos of great length.

For at the side opposite to the sepulcher, which was the eastern side, the church itself was erected; a noble work rising to a vast height, and of great extent both in length and breadth. The interior of this structure was floored with marble slabs of various colors while the external surface of the walls, which shone with polished stones exactly fitted together, exhibited a degree of splendor in no respect of inferior to that of marble. With regard to the roof, it was covered on the outside with lead, as a protection against the rains of winter. But the inner part of the roof, which was finished with sculptured fretwork, extended in a series of connected compartments, like a vast sea, over the whole church, and being overlaid throughout with the purest gold, caused the entire building to glitter as it were with rays of light.

Besides this were two porticos on each side, with upper and lower ranges of pillars, corresponding in length with the church itself; and these also had their roofs ornamented with gold. Of these porticos, those which were exterior to the church, were supported by columns of great size, while those within these, rested on piles[15] of stone beautifully adorned on the surface. Three gates, placed exactly east, were intended to receive those who entered the church.

Opposite these gates the crowning part of the whole was the hemisphere,[16] which rose to the very summit of the church. This was encircled by twelve columns, (according to the number of the apostles of our Savior,) having their capitals embellished with silver bowls of great size, which the emperor himself presented as a splendid offering to his God.

In the next place he enclosed the atrium, which occupied the space leading to the entrances in front of the church. This comprehended, first the court, then the porticos on each side, and lastly the gates of the court. After these, in the midst of the open marketplace,[17] the entrance gates of the whole work, which were of exquisite workmanship, afforded to passers-by on the outside a view of the interior which could not fail to inspire astonishment.

CHAPTER XXX
OF THE NUMBER OF HIS OFFERINGS.

This temple, then, the emperor erected a conspicuous monument of the Savior's resurrection, and embellished it throughout on an imperial scale of magnificence. He further enriched it with numberless offerings of inexpressible beauty, consisting of gold, silver, and precious stones, in various forms; the skilful and elaborate arrangement of which, in regard to their magnitude, number, and variety, we have not leisure at present to describe particularly.

CHAPTER XXXI
OF THE ERECTION OF CHURCHES IN BETHLEHEM, AND ON THE MOUNT OF OLIVES.

In the same country he discovered other places, venerable as being the localities of two sacred caves, and these also he adorned with lavish magnificence. In the one case, he rendered due honor to that which had been the scene of the first manifestation of our Savior's divine presence, when He submitted to be born in mortal flesh, while in the case of the second cavern he hallowed the remembrance of His ascension to heaven from the mountain top. And while he at the same time eternized the memory of his mother, who had been the instrument of conferring so valuable a benefit on mankind.

CHAPTER XXXII

THAT HELENA AUGUSTA, CONSTANTINE'S MOTHER, HAVING VISITED THIS LOCALITY FOR DEVOTIONAL PURPOSES, BUILT THESE CHURCHES.

For this empress, having resolved to discharge the duties of pious devotion to the Supreme God, and feeling it incumbent on her to render thanksgivings with prayers on behalf both of her own son, now so mighty an emperor, and of his sons, her own grandchildren, the divinely favored Cæsars, with youthful alacrity (though now advanced in years, yet gifted with no common degree of wisdom), had hastened to survey this venerable land, and at the same time to visit the eastern provinces, cities, and people, with a truly imperial solicitude. As soon, then, as she had rendered due reverence to the ground which the Savior's feet had trodden, according to the prophetic word which says, "Let us worship at the place whereon His feet have stood,"[18] she immediately bequeathed the fruit of her piety to future generations.

CHAPTER XXXIII

A FURTHER NOTICE OF THE CHURCHES AT BETHLEHEM.

For without delay she dedicated two churches to the God whom she adored—one at the grotto which had been the scene of the Savior's birth, the other on the mount of His ascension. For He who was "God with us" had submitted to be born even in a cave[19] of the earth, and the place of His nativity was called Bethlehem by the Hebrews. Accordingly the pious empress honored with rare memorials the scene of her travail who bore this heavenly child, and beautified the sacred cave with all possible splendor. The emperor for the spot by princely offerings, and added to mother's magnificence by costly presents of silver and gold, and embroidered curtains. Once more, his imperial mother raised a stately structure on the Mount of Olives also, in memory of His ascent to heaven who is the Savior of mankind, erecting a sacred church or temple on the very summit of the mount. And indeed authentic history informs us that in a cave on this very spot the Savior imparted mysterious and secret revelations to His disciples.[20] And here also the emperor testified his reverence for the King of kings, by diverse and costly offerings. Thus did Helena Augusta, the pious mother of a pious emperor, erect these two noble and beautiful monuments of devotion, worthy of everlasting remembrance, to the honor of God her Savior, and as proofs of her holy zeal. And thus did she receive from her son the countenance and aid of his imperial power. Nor was it long ere this aged lady reaped the due reward of her labors. After passing the whole period of her life, even to declining age, in the greatest prosperity, and exhibiting both in word and deed abundant fruits of obedience to the divine precepts, and having enjoyed in consequence an easy and tranquil existence, with unimpaired powers of body and mind, at length she obtained from God an end befitting her pious course, and a recompense of her good deeds even in this present life.

CHAPTER XXXIV

OF HELENA'S GENEROSITY AND BENEFICENT ACTS.

For on the occasion of a circuit which she made of the eastern provinces, with circumstances of royal splendor, she bestowed abundant proofs of her liberality as well on the inhabitants of the several cities collectively, as on individuals who approached her, at the same time that she scattered largesses among the soldiery with a liberal hand. But especially abundant were the gifts she bestowed on the naked and friendless poor. To some she gave money, to others an ample supply of clothing. She liberated some from imprisonment, or from the bitter servitude of the mines. Others she delivered from unjust oppression, and others again, she restored from exile to their native land.

CHAPTER XXXV

HER PIOUS CONDUCT IN THE CHURCHES.

While, however, her character derived luster from such deeds as I have described, she was far from neglecting personal piety toward God. She might be seen continually frequenting His Church. While at the same time she adorned the houses of prayer with splendid offerings, not overlooking the churches of the smallest cities. In short, this admirable woman was to be seen, in simple and modest attire, mingling with the crowd of worshippers, and testifying her devotion to God by a uniform course of pious conduct.

CHAPTER XXXVI

SHE MAKES HER WILL, AND DIES AT THE AGE OF EIGHTY YEARS.

And when at length, at the close of a long life, she was called to inherit a happier lot, having arrived at the eightieth year of her age, and being very near the time of her departure, she prepared and executed her last will in favor of her only son, the emperor and sole monarch of the world, and her grandchildren, the Cæsars his sons, to whom severally she bequeathed whatever property she possessed in any part of the world. Having thus disposed of her earthly affairs, this thrice blessed woman breathed her last in the presence of her illustrious son, who was in attendance at her side, and clasped her hands, so that, to those who rightly discerned the truth, she seemed to experience a real change and transition from an earthly to a heavenly existence, since her soul, remolded as it were into an incorruptible and angelic essence,[21] was received up into her Savior's presence.

CHAPTER XXXVII

HOW CONSTANTINE BURIED HIS MOTHER, AND HOW HE HONORED HER DURING HER LIFE.

Her body, too, was honored with special tokens of respect, being escorted on its way to the imperial city by a vast train of guards, and there deposited in a royal tomb. Such were the last days of our emperor's mother, a person worthy of being held in perpetual remembrance, both for her own practical piety, and because she had given birth to so extraordinary and admirable an offspring. And well may his character be styled blessed, for his filial piety as well as on other grounds. He rendered her through his influence so devout a worshipper of God (though not previously so), that she seemed to have been instructed from the first by the Savior of mankind. And besides this, he had honored her so fully with imperial dignities, that in every province, and in the very ranks of the soldiery, she was spoken of under the titles of Augusta, and empress, and her likeness was impressed on golden coins. He had even granted her authority over the imperial treasures, to use and dispense them according to her own will and discretion in every case, for this enviable distinction also she received at the hands of her son.

Hence it is that among the qualities which shed a luster

on his memory, we may rightly include that surpassing degree of filial affection whereby he rendered full obedience to the Divine precepts which enjoin due honor from children to their parents. In this manner, then, the emperor executed in Palestine the noble works I have above described, and indeed in every province he raised new churches on a far more imposing scale than those which had existed before his time.

CHAPTER XXXVIII

HE BUILDS CHURCHES IN HONOR OF MARTYRS, AND ABOLISHES IDOLATRY AT CONSTANTINOPLE.

And being fully resolved to distinguish the city which bore his name with especial honor, he embellished it with numerous sacred edifices, both memorials of martyrs on the largest scale, and other buildings of the most splendid kind. Not only within the city itself, but in its vicinity: and thus at the same time he rendered honor to the memory of the martyrs, and consecrated his city to the martyrs' God. Being filled, too, with Divine wisdom, he determined to purge the city which was to be distinguished by his own name from idolatry of every kind, that henceforth no statues might be worshipped there in the temples of those falsely reputed to be gods, nor any altars defiled by the pollution of blood—that there might be no sacrifices consumed by fire, no demon festivals, nor any of the other ceremonies usually observed by the slaves of superstition.[22]

CHAPTER XXXIX

PRESENTATION OF THE CROSS IN THE PALACE, AND OF DANIEL AT THE PUBLIC FOUNTAINS.

On the other hand one might see the fountains in the midst of the forum graced with figures representing the good

Shepherd (well known to those who study the sacred oracles), and that of Daniel also with the lions, forged in brass, and resplendent with plates of gold. Indeed, so large a measure of Divine love possessed the emperor's soul, that in the principal apartment of the imperial palace itself, on a vast tablet displayed in the center of its gilded ceiling, he caused the symbol of our Savior's Passion to be fixed, composed of a variety of precious stones richly inwrought with gold. And this symbol the pious prince seemed to have intended to be as it were the safeguard of the empire itself.

CHAPTER XL

HE ERECTS CHURCHES IN NICOMEDIA, AND IN OTHER CITIES.

Having thus embellished the city which bore his name, he next distinguished the metropolis of Bithynia[23] by the erection of a stately and magnificent church, being desirous of raising in this city also, in honor of his Savior and at his own charges, a memorial of his victory over his own enemies and the adversaries of God. He also decorated the principal cities of the other provinces with sacred edifices of great beauty as, for example, in the case of that metropolis of the East which derived its name from Antiochus, in which, as the head of that portion of the empire, he consecrated to the service of God a church of unparalleled size and beauty. The entire building was encompassed by an enclosure of great extent within which the church itself rose to a vast elevation being of an octagonal form, and surrounded on all sides by many chambers, courts, and upper and lower apartments; the whole richly adorned with a profusion of gold, brass, and other materials of the most costly kind.

CHAPTER XLI

HE ORDERS A CHURCH TO BE BUILT AT MAMBRE.

Such were the principal sacred edifices erected by the emperor's command. But having heard that the self-same Savior who erewhile had appeared on earth had in ages long since past afforded a manifestation of His Divine presence to holy men of Palestine near the oak of Mambre,[24] he ordered that a house of prayer should be built there also in honor of the God who had thus appeared. Accordingly the imperial commission was transmitted to the provincial governors by letters addressed to them individually, enjoining a speedy completion of the appointed work. He sent moreover to the writer of this history an eloquent admonition, a copy of which I think it well to insert in the present work, in order to convey a just idea of his pious diligence and zeal. To express, then, his displeasure at the evil practices which he had heard were usual in the place just referred to, he addressed me in the following terms.

CHAPTER XLII

CONSTANTINE'S LETTER TO EUSEBIUS CONCERNING MAMBRE.

Victor Constantinus, Maximus Augustus, to Macarius, and the rest of the bishops in Palestine.

One benefit, and that of no ordinary importance, has been conferred on us by my truly pious mother-in-law,[25] in that she has made known to us by letter that abandoned folly of impious men which has hitherto escaped detection by you—so that the criminal conduct this overlooked may now obtain, through our means, that attention and correction which are absolutely needed, however tardily applied. For surely it is a grave impiety indeed, that holy places should be defiled by the stain of unhallowed impurities. What then is this, dearest brethren, which, though it has eluded your Sagacity, she of whom I speak was impelled by a pious sense of duty to disclose?

She assures me, then, that the place which takes its name from the oak of Mambre, where we find that Abraham dwelt, is defiled by certain of the slaves of superstition in every possible way. She declares that idols which should be utterly destroyed have been erected on the site of that tree, that an altar is near the spot, and that impure sacrifices are continually performed. Now since it is evident that these practices are equally inconsistent with the character of our times, and unworthy the sanctity of the place itself, I wish your Gravities to be informed that the illustrious Count Acacius, our friend, has received instructions by letter from me, to the effect that every idol which shall be found in the place above-mentioned shall immediately be consigned to the flames, that the altar be utterly demolished, and that if any one, after this our mandate, shall be guilty of impiety of any kind in this place, he shall be visited with condign punishment. The place itself we have directed to be adorned with an unpolluted structure—I mean a church—in order that it may become a fitting place of assembly for holy men. Meantime, should any breach of these our commands occur, it should be made known to our clemency without the least delay by letters from you, that we may direct the person detected to be dealt with, as a transgressor of the law, in the severest manner. For you are not ignorant that the Supreme God first appeared to Abraham, and conversed with him, in that place. There it was that the observance of the Divine law first began; there first the Savior Himself, with the two angels, vouchsafed to Abraham a manifestation of His presence; there God first appeared to men; there He gave promise to Abraham concerning his future seed, and straightway fulfilled that promise; there He foretold that he should be the father of a multitude of nations. For these reasons, it seems to me right that this place should not only be kept pure through our diligence from all defilement, but restored also to its pristine sanctity, that nothing hereafter may be done there except the performance of fitting service to Him who is the Almighty God, and our Savior, and Lord of all. And this service it is incumbent on you to care for with due attention, if your Gravities be willing (and of this I feel confident), to gratify my wishes, which are especially interested in the worship of God.

May He preserve you, beloved brethren!

CHAPTER XLIII

THE IDOL TEMPLES AND IMAGES EVERYWHERE DESTROYED.

All these things the emperor diligently performed to the praise of the saving power of Christ, and thus made it his constant aim to glorify his Savior God. On the other hand he used every means to rebuke the superstitious errors of the heathen. Hence the entrances of their temples in the several cities were left exposed to the weather, being stripped of their doors at his command. The tiling of others was removed, and their roofs destroyed. From others again the venerable statues of brass, of which the superstition of antiquity had boasted for a long series of years, were exposed to view in all the public places of the imperial city: so that here a Pythian, there a Sminthian Apollo, excited the contempt of the beholder, while the Delphic tripods were deposited in the circus, and the Muses of Helicon in the palace itself.

In short, the city of Constantinople was everywhere filled with brazen statues of the most exquisite workmanship, which had been dedicated in every province, and which the deluded victims of superstition had long vainly honored as gods with numberless victims and burnt sacrifices, though now at length they learnt to renounce their error, when the emperor held up the very objects of their worship to be the ridicule and sport of all beholders. With regard to those images which were of gold, he dealt with them in a different manner. For as soon as he understood that the ignorant multitudes were inspired with a vain and childish dread of these bugbears of error, wrought in gold and silver, he judged it right to remove these also (like stumbling-stones thrown in the way of men walking in the dark), and henceforward to open a plain and unobstructed road to all.

Having formed this resolution, he considered no military force needful for the repression of the evil. A few of his own friends sufficed for this service, and these he sent by a simple expression of his will to visit each several province. Accordingly, sustained by confidence in the emperor's pious intentions and their own personal devotion to God, they passed through the midst of numberless tribes and nations, abolishing this ancient error in every city and country. They ordered the priests themselves, amidst general laughter and scorn, to bring their gods from their dark recesses to the light of day. They then stripped them of their ornaments, and exhibited to the gaze of all the unsightly reality which had been hidden beneath a painted exterior. Lastly, whatever part of the material appeared valuable they scraped off and melted in the fire to prove its worth, after which they secured and set apart whatever they judged needful for their purpose, leaving to the superstitious worshippers that which was altogether useless, as a memorial of their shame. Meanwhile our admirable prince was himself engaged in a work similar to what we have described. For at the same time that these costly images of the dead were stripped, as we have said, of their precious materials, he also attacked those composed of brass; causing those to be dragged from their places with ropes and as it were carried away captive, whom the dotage of antiquity had esteemed as gods.

CHAPTER XLIV

OVERTHROW OF AN IDOL TEMPLE, AND ABOLITION OF LICENTIOUS PRACTICES, AT APHACA IN PHŒNICIA.

The emperor's next care was to kindle, as it were, a brilliant torch, by the light of which he directed his imperial gaze around, to see if any hidden vestiges of error might still exist. And as the keen-sighted eagle in its heavenward flight, is able to descry from its lofty height the most distant objects on the earth, so did he, while residing in the imperial palace of his own fair city, discover as from a watch-tower a hidden and fatal snare of souls in the province of Phœnicia. This was a grove and temple, not situated in the midst of any city, nor in any public place (as mostly is the case with a view to splendor of effect), but apart from the beaten and frequented road, at Aphaca, on part of the summit of Mount Libanus, and dedicated to the foul demon known by the name Venus. It was a school of wickedness for all votaries of sensuality and impurity. Here men undeserving of the name forgot the dignity of their sex, and propitiated the demon by their effeminate conduct. Here too unlawful commerce of women and adulterous intercourse, with other horrible and infamous practices, were perpetrated in this temple as in a place beyond the scope and restraint of law.

Meantime these evils remained unchecked by the presence of any observer, since no one of fair character ventured to visit such scenes. These proceedings, however, could not escape the vigilance of our august emperor, who, having himself inspected them with characteristic forethought, and judging that such a temple was unfit for the light of heaven, gave orders that the building with its offerings should be utterly destroyed. Accordingly, in obedience to the imperial command, these engines of an abandoned superstition were immediately abolished, and the hand of military force was made instrumental in purging the impurities of the place. And now those who had heretofore lived without restraint found an inducement to modesty in the emperor's threat of punishment, as did also those superstitious Gentiles who had boasted in their fancied wisdom, but now obtained experimental proof of their own vanity and folly.

CHAPTER XLV

DESTRUCTION OF THE TEMPLE OF ÆSCULAPIUS AT ÆGÆ.[26]

For since it happened that many of these pretenders to wisdom were deluded votaries of the demon worshipped in Cilicia, whom thousands regarded with reverence as the possessor of saving and healing power, who sometimes appeared to those who passed the night in his temple, sometimes restored the diseased to health (though in reality he was a destroyer of souls, who drew his easily deluded worshippers from the true Savior to involve them in impious error), the emperor, consistently with his practice and desire to advance the worship of Him who is at once a jealous God and the true Savior, gave directions that this temple also should be razed to the ground. In prompt obedience to this command, a band of soldiers laid this building, the object of admiration even to noble philosophers, prostrate in the dust, together with its unseen inmate, neither demon nor god, but rather a deceiver of souls, who had seduced mankind for so long a series of years. And thus he who had promised to others deliverance from misfortune and distress, could find no means for his own security, any more than when (as fables feign) he was scorched by the lightning's stroke.[27] Our emperor's pious deeds, however, had in them nothing fabulous or feigned, but by virtue of the manifested power of his Savior, this temple as well as others was so utterly overthrown, that not a vestige of the former follies was left behind.

CHAPTER XLVI

HOW THE GENTILES ABANDONED IDOL WORSHIP, AND TURNED TO THE KNOWLEDGE OF GOD.

Hence it was that, of those who had been the slaves of superstition, when they saw with their own eyes the exposure of the delusion by which they had been enthralled, and beheld the actual ruin of the temples and images in every place, some themselves to the saving doctrine of Christ, while others, though they declined to take this step, yet reprobated the senseless creed of their fathers, and laughed those falsities to scorn, which they had so long been accustomed to regard as gods. Indeed, what other feelings could possess their minds, when they witnessed the thorough uncleanness concealed beneath the fair exterior of the objects of their worship? Beneath this were found either the bones of dead men or dry skulls, fraudulently obtained by designing impostors, or filthy rags full of abominable impurity, or a bundle of hay or stubble. On seeing all these things heaped together within their lifeless images, they denounced their fathers' folly and their own, especially when neither in the secret recesses of the temples nor in the statues themselves could any inmate be found—neither demon, nor utterer of oracles, neither god nor prophet, as they had heretofore supposed. Nay, not even a dim and shadowy phantom could be seen. Accordingly, every gloomy cavern, every hidden recess, afforded easy access to the emperor's emissaries. The inaccessible and secret chambers, the innermost shrines of the temples, were trampled by the soldiers' feet, and thus the mental blindness which had prevailed for so many ages over the gentile world became clearly apparent to the eyes of all.

CHAPTER XLVII

CONSTANTINE DESTROYS THE TEMPLE OF VENUS AT HELIOPOLIS, AND BUILDS THE FIRST CHURCH IN THAT CITY.

Such actions as I have described may well be reckoned among the emperor's noblest achievements, as also the wise arrangements which he made respecting each particular province. We may instance the Phœnician city Heliopolis, in which those who dignify licentious pleasure with a distinguishing title of honor, had permitted their wives and daughters to commit shameless fornication. But now a new statute, breathing the very spirit of modesty, proceeded from the emperor, which peremptorily forbade the continuance of former practices. And besides this, he sent them also written exhortations, as though he had been especially ordained by God for this end, that he might instruct all men in the principles of charity. Hence, he disdained not to communicate by letter even with these persons, urging them to seek diligently the knowledge of God.

At the same time he followed up his words by corresponding deeds, and erected even in this city a church of great size and magnificence, so that an event unheard of before in any age, now for the first time came to pass— namely, that a city which had hitherto been wholly given up to superstition now obtained the privilege of a church of God, with presbyters and deacons. And its deacons, and its people were placed under the presiding care of a bishop consecrated the service of the supreme God. And further, the emperor, being anxious that here also as many possible might be won to the profession of the truth, bestowed abundant provision for the necessities of the poor, desiring even thus to invite them to seek the doctrines of salvation, as though he were almost adopting the words of him who said, "Whether in pretence, or in truth, let Christ be preached."[28]

CHAPTER XLVIII

OF THE DISTURBANCES RAISED AT ANTIOCH ON ACCOUNT OF EUSTATHIUS.

In the midst, however, of the general happiness occasioned by these events, and while the Church of God was every where and every way flourishing throughout the empire, once more that spirit of envy, who ever watches for the ruin of the good, prepared himself to combat the greatness of our prosperity, in the expectation, perhaps, that the emperor himself, provoked by our tumults and disorders, might eventually become estranged from us. Accordingly, he kindled a furious controversy at Antioch, and thereby involved the church in that place in a series of tragic calamities, which had well nigh occasioned the total overthrow of the city. The members of the Church were divided into two opposite parties, while the people, including even the magistrates and soldiery, regarded each other with feelings of bitter hostility, so that the contest would have been decided by the sword, had not the watchful providence of God, as well as dread of the emperor's displeasure, controlled the fury of the multitude.

On this occasion too, the emperor, acting the part of a preserver and physician of souls, applied with much forbearance the remedy of persuasion to those who needed it. He gently pleaded, as it were, by an embassy with his people, sending among them one of the best approved and most faithful of those who were honored with the dignity of Count. At the same time, he exhorted them to a peaceable spirit by repeated letters, and instructed them in the practice of true godliness. Having prevailed by these remonstrances, he excused their conduct in his subsequent letters, alleging that he had himself heard the merits of the case from him on whose account the disturbance had arisen.[29] And these letters of his, which are replete with learning and instruction of no ordinary kind, I should have inserted in this present work, were it not that they might affix a mark of dishonor to the character of the persons accused. I will therefore omit these, being unwilling to revive the memory of past grievances, and will only annex those to my present narrative which he wrote to testify his satisfaction at the re-establishment of peace and concord among the rest. In the letters, he cautioned them against any desire to claim the ruler of another district as their own (through whose intervention peace had been restored), and exhorted them, consistently with the usage of the Church, to choose him as their bishop, whom the common Savior of all should point out as suited for the office.

146

His letter, then, is addressed to the people and to the bishops, severally, in the following terms.

CHAPTER XLIX

CONSTANTINE'S LETTER TO THE ANTIOCHIANS, DIRECTING THEM NOT TO WITHDRAW EUSEBIUS FROM CÆSAREA, BUT TO SEEK FOR ANOTHER BISHOP.

Victor Constantinus, Maximus Augustus, to the people of Antioch.

How pleasing to the wise and intelligent portion of mankind is the concord which exists among you! And I myself, brethren, am disposed to love you with an enduring affection, inspired both by religion and by your own manner of life and zeal on my behalf. It is by the exercise of right understanding and sound discretion, that we are enabled really to enjoy our blessings. And what can become you so well as this discretion? No wonder, then, if I affirm that your maintenance of the truth has tended rather to promote your security than to draw on you the hatred of others. Indeed, amongst brethren, whom the selfsame disposition to walk in the ways of truth and righteousness promises, through the favor of God, to register among His pure and holy family, what can be more honorable than gladly to acquiesce in the prosperity of all men? Especially since the precepts of the Divine law prescribe a better direction to your proposed intention, and we ourselves desire that your judgment should be confirmed by proper sanction.

It may be that you are surprised, and at a loss to understand the meaning of this introduction to my present address. The cause of it I will not hesitate to explain without reserve. I confess, then, that on reading your records I perceived, by the highly eulogistic testimony which they bear to Eusebius bishop of Cæsarea (whom I have myself long well known and esteemed for his learning and moderation), that you are strongly attached to him and desire to appropriate him as your own prelate. What thoughts, then, do you suppose that I entertain on this subject, desirous as I am to seek for and act on the strict principles of right? What anxiety do you imagine this desire of yours has caused me? O holy faith, who givest us in our Savior's words and precepts a model, as it were, of what our life should be, how hardly wouldst thou thyself resist the course of sin, were it not that thou refusest to subserve the purposes of gain! In my own judgment, he whose first object is the maintenance of peace, seems to be superior to Victory herself, and where a right and honorable course lies open to one's choice, surely no one would hesitate to adopt it.

I ask then, brethren, why do we so decide as to inflict an injury on others by our choice? Why do we covet those objects which will destroy the credit of our own character? I myself highly esteem the individual whom ye judge worthy of your respect and affection. Notwithstanding, it cannot be right that those principles should be entirely disregarded which should be authoritative and binding on all alike—for example, that each should be content with the limits assigned them, and that all should enjoy their proper privileges. Nor can it be right in considering the claims of rival candidates, to suppose but that not one only, but many, may appear worthy of comparison with this person. For as long as no violence or harshness are suffered to disturb the dignities of the church, they continue to be on an equal footing, and worthy of the same consideration everywhere. Nor is it reasonable that an inquiry into the qualifications of one person should be made to the detriment of others, since the judgment of all churches, whether reckoned of greater or less importance in themselves, is equally capable of receiving and maintaining the Divine ordinances, so that one is in no way inferior to another (if we will but boldly declare the truth), in regard to that standard of practice which is common to all.

If this be so, we must say that you will be chargeable, not with retaining this prelate, but with wrongfully removing him, your conduct will be characterized rather by violence than justice, and whatever may be generally thought by others, I dare clearly and boldly affirm that this measure will furnish ground of accusation against you, and will provoke factious disturbances of the most mischievous kind. For even timid flocks can shew the use and power of their teeth when the watchful care of their shepherd declines, and they find themselves bereft of his accustomed guidance.

If this then be really so, if I am not deceived in my judgment, let this, brethren, be your first consideration (for many and important considerations will immediately present them-selves, if you adopt my advice), whether, should you persist in your intention, that mutual kindly feeling and affection which should subsist among you will suffer no diminution? In the next place, remember that Eusebius, who came among you for the purpose of offering disinterested counsel, now enjoys the reward which is due to him in the judgment of heaven. For he has received no ordinary recompense in the high testimony you have borne to his equitable conduct.

Lastly, in accordance with your usual sound judgment, do ye exhibit a becoming diligence in selecting the person of whom you stand in need, carefully avoiding all factious and tumultuous clamor—for such clamor is always wrong, and from the collision of discordant elements both sparks and flame will arise. I protest, as I desire to please God and you, and to enjoy a happiness commensurate with your kind wishes, that I love you, and the quiet haven of your gentleness, now that you have cast from you that which defiled,[30] and received in its place at once sound morality and concord, firmly planting in the vessel the sacred standard, and guided, as one may say, by a helm of iron in your course onward to the light of heaven. Receive then on board that merchandise which is incorruptible, since all impurity has been drained, as it were, from the vessel, and be careful henceforth so to secure the enjoyment of all your present blessing, that you may not seem at any future time either to have determined any measure on the impulse of inconsiderate or ill-directed zeal, or in the first instance rashly to have entered on an inexpedient course.

May God preserve you, beloved brethren!

CHAPTER L

THE EMPEROR'S LETTER TO EUSEBIUS, ON THE OCCASION OF HIS REFUSING THE BISHOPRIC OF ANTIOCH.

Victor Constantinus, Maximus Augustus, to Eusebius.

I have most carefully perused your letter, and perceive that you have strictly conformed to the rule enjoined by the discipline of the Church. Now to abide by that which appears at the same time pleasing to God, and accordant with apostolical tradition, is a proof of true piety. And you have reason to deem yourself happy on this behalf, that you are counted worthy, in the judgment, I may say, of all the world, to have the oversight of the whole Church. For the desire which all feel to claim you for their own, undoubtedly enhances your enviable fortune in this respect. Notwithstanding, your Prudence, whose resolve it is to observe the ordinances of God and the apostolic rule of the church, has done excellently well in declining the bishopric of the Church at Antioch, and desiring to continue in that Church of which you first received the oversight by the will of God.

I have written on this subject to the people of Antioch, and also to your colleagues in the ministry who had themselves consulted me in regard to this question, on reading which letters, your Holiness will easily discern, that (inasmuch as justice itself opposed their claims) I have written to them under divine direction. It will be necessary that your Prudence should be present at their conference, in order that this decision may be ratified in the Church at Antioch.

God preserve you, beloved brother!

CHAPTER LI

CONSTANTINE'S LETTER TO THE COUNCIL, DEPRECATING THE REMOVAL OF EUSEBIUS FROM CÆSAREA.

Victor Constantinus, Maximus Augustus, to Theodotus, Theodorus, Narcissus, Ætius, Alpheus, and the rest of the bishops who are at Antioch.

I have perused the letters written by your Prudences, and highly approve of the wise resolution of your colleague in the ministry, Eusebius. Having, moreover, been informed of the circumstances of the case, partly by your letters, partly by those of our illustrious friends Acacius and Strategius, after sufficient investigation I have written to the people of Antioch, suggesting the course which will be at once pleasing to God and advantageous for the Church. A copy of this I have ordered to be subjoined to this present letter, in order that ye yourselves may know what I thought fit, as an advocate of the cause of justice, to write to that people, since I find in your letter this proposal, that, in consonance with the choice of the people, sanctioned by your own desire, Eusebius the holy bishop of Cæsarea should preside over and take the charge of the Church at Antioch.

Now the letters of Eusebius himself on this subject appeared to be strictly accordant with the order prescribed by the Church. Nevertheless it is expedient that your Prudences should be made acquainted with my opinion also. For I am informed that Euphronius the presbyter, who is a citizen of Cæsarea in Cappadocia, and George of Arethusa, likewise a presbyter, and appointed to that office by Alexander at Alexandria,[31] are men of tried faith. It was right, therefore, to intimate to your Prudences, that in proposing these men and any others whom you may deem worthy the episcopal dignity, you should decide this question in a manner conformable to the tradition of the apostles. For in that case, your Prudences will be able, according to the rule of the Church and apostolic tradition, to direct this election in the manner which true ecclesiastical discipline shall prescribe.

God preserve you, beloved brethren!

CHAPTER LII

HOW HE DISPLAYED HIS ZEAL FOR THE EXTIRPATION OF HERESIES.

Such were the exhortations to maintain the integrity of the divine religion which the emperor addressed to the rulers of the churches. Having by these means banished dissension, and reduced the Church of God to a happy uniformity of doctrine, he next proceeded to a different duty, feeling it incumbent on him to extirpate another sort of impious persons, as pernicious enemies of the human race. These were pests of society, who ruined whole cities under the specious garb of religious decorum—men whom our Savior's warning voice somewhere terms false prophets and ravenous wolves: "Beware of false prophets, who will come to you in sheep's clothing, but inwardly they are ravening wolves. Ye shall know them by their fruits."[32] Accordingly, by an order transmitted to the governors of the several provinces, he effectually banished all such offenders. In addition to this ordinance he addressed to them personally a severely awakening admonition, exhorting them to an earnest repentance, that they might still find a haven of safety in the true Church of God. Hear, then, in what manner he addressed them in this letter.

CHAPTER LIII

CONSTANTINE'S EDICT AGAINST THE HERETICS.

Victor Constantinus, Maximus Augustus, to the heretics.

Understand now, by this present statute, ye Novatians, Valentinians, Marcionites, Paulians, ye who are called Cataphrygians, and all ye who devise and support heresies by means of your private assemblies, with what a tissue of falsehood and vanity, with what destructive and venomous errors, your doctrines are inseparably interwoven, so that through you the healthy soul is stricken with disease, and the living becomes the prey of everlasting death. Ye haters and enemies of truth and life, in league with destruction! All your counsels are opposed to the truth, but familiar with deeds of baseness, fit subjects for the fabulous follies of the stage. And by these ye frame falsehoods, oppress the innocent, and withhold the light from them that believe. Ever trespassing under the mask of godliness, ye fill all things with defilement. Ye pierce the pure and guileless conscience with deadly wounds, while ye withdraw, one may almost say, the very light of day from the eyes of men.

But why should I particularize, when to speak of your criminality as it deserves demands more time and leisure than I can give? For so long and unmeasured is the catalogue of your offences, so hateful and altogether atrocious are they, that a single day would not suffice to recount them all. And indeed it is well to turn one's ears and eyes from such a subject, lest by a description of each particular evil, the pure sincerity and freshness of one's own faith be impaired. Why then do I still bear with such abounding evil, especially since this protracted clemency is the cause that some who were sound are become tainted with this pestilent disease? Why not at once strike, as it were, at the root of so great a mischief by a public manifestation of displeasure?

Forasmuch, then, as it is no longer possible to bear with your pernicious errors, we give warning by this present statute that none of you henceforth presume to assemble yourselves together. We have directed, accordingly, that you be deprived of all the houses in which you are accustomed to hold your assemblies, and our care in this respect extends so far as to forbid the holding of your superstitious and senseless meetings, not in public merely, but in any private house or place whatsoever.

Let those of you, therefore, who are desirous of embracing the true and pure religion, take the far better course of entering the Catholic Church, and uniting with it in holy fellowship, whereby you will be enabled to arrive at the knowledge of the truth. In any case, the delusions of your perverted understandings must entirely cease to mingle with and mar the felicity of our present times—I mean the impious and wretched double-mindedness of heretics and schismatics. For it is an object worthy of that prosperity which we enjoy through the favor of God, to endeavor to bring back those who in time past were living in the hope of future blessing, from all irregularity and error to the right path, from darkness to light, from vanity to truth, from death to salvation.

And in order that this remedy may be applied with effectual power, we have commanded (as before said), that you be positively deprived of every gathering point for your superstitious meetings, I mean all the houses of prayer (if such be worthy of the name) which belong to heretics, and that these be made over without delay to the Catholic Church, that any other places be confiscated to the public service, and no facility whatever be left for any future gathering. In order that from this day forward none of your unlawful assemblies may presume to appear in any public or private place, let this edict be made public.

CHAPTER LIV

ON THE DISCOVERY OF PROHIBITED BOOKS AMONG THE HERETICS, MANY OF THEM RETURN TO THE CATHOLIC CHURCH.

Thus were the lurking-places of the heretics broken up by the emperor's command, and the savage beasts they harbored (I mean the chief authors of their impious doctrines) driven to flight. Of those whom they had deceived, some, intimidated by the emperor's threats, with a false and time-serving disguise of their real sentiments, crept secretly into the Church. For since the law directed that search should be made for their books, those of them who practiced evil and forbidden arts were detected, and these were ready to secure their own safety by dissimulation of every kind. Others, however, there were who voluntarily and with real sincerity embraced a better hope.

Meantime the prelates of the several churches continued to make strict inquiry, utterly rejecting those who attempted an entrance under the specious disguise of false pretenses, while those who came with sincerity of purpose were proved for a time, and after sufficient trial numbered with the congregation, such was the treatment of those who stood charged with rank heresy. Those, however, who maintained no impious doctrine, but had been separated from the one body through the influence of schismatic advisers, were received without difficulty or delay. Accordingly, numbers thus revisited (as it were) their own country after an absence in a foreign land, and acknowledged the Church as a mother from whom they had wandered long, and to whom they now returned with joy and gladness.

Thus the members of the entire body became united, and compacted in one harmonious whole, and the one Catholic Church, at unity with itself, shone with full luster, while no heretical or schismatic body anywhere continued to exist. And the credit of having achieved this mighty work our Heaven-protected emperor alone, of all who had gone before him, was able to attribute to himself.

NOTES

1. Πολιτευτῶν ἀνδρῶν, here, apparently, the Decurions, who formed the corporations of the cities, and were subject to responsible burdensome offices. See Gibbon, *Decline and Fall*, chap. xvii.
2. Literally, by encaustic painting. See Book I, note 2, p. 46 of the present volume.
3. *Note to the 2009 edition:* Symplegades: the famous "clashing rocks" of Greek mythology.
4. Hosius of Cordova.
5. It has been doubted whether Rome or Constantinople is intended. The authority of Sozomen and others is in favor of the former. See *Ecclesiastical History*, p. 39. *Note to the 2009 edition:* The

Liber Pontificalis seems to support this claim, maintaining that Constantine called the Council of Nicaea, either with the approval or at the bidding of Pope Sylvester (p. 44). It says nothing, however, about his attendance at the council, mentioning only that 208 bishops who were unable to attend, sent their signatures.

6. *Note to the 2009 edition:* This passage parallels a description of the first Pentecost taken from Acts 2:5–11.

7. Hence it seems probable that this was the last day of the Council, the entire session of which occupied more than two months, and which was originally held in a church.

8. The authority of Sozomen and other writers seems to decide that this was Eusebius himself.

9. The idea seems to be (as explained by Valesius) that if they joined the Jews in celebrating this feast, they would seem to consent to their crime in crucifying the Lord.

10. Ἀγχίνοια. This word is one of a class of expressions frequently used by Eusebius, and which, being intended as titles of honor, like "Excellency," etc. should, where possible, be thus rendered. In the present instance it is applied to the heads of the churches collectively.

11. Valesius explains this as referring to the conduct of the Jews in professing to acknowledge God as their king, and yet denying Him by saying, "We have no king but Cæsar."

12. Licinius appears to be meant, whose death had occurred AD 326, in which year the alleged discovery of the Lord's sepulcher took place.

13. Apparently referring (says Valesius) to Revelations 21:2:—"And I, John, saw the holy city, new Jerusalem, coming down from God, out of heaven," etc.: an extraordinary application of Scripture, though perhaps characteristic of the author's age.

14. *Note to the 2009 edition:* The description of the Church of the Holy Sepulcher was broken up in the previous edition by chapter titles inserted by a later copyist. As these titles are, in most cases, nearly as long as the text they described and were not otherwise of any utility, they have been removed here. See note 10, p. 98 of the present volume.

15. These inner porticos seem to have rested on massy piles, because they adjoined the sides of the church, and had to bear its roof, which was loftier than any of the rest.

16. Apparently, the altar, which was of a hemispherical, or rather hemicylindrical form.

17. In front of the larger churches there was generally a street or open space, where a market was held on the festival of the Martyr to whom

the church was dedicated. Regard was also had in this arrangement, to architectural effect, the object being that nothing should interfere with the view of the front of the church. Vide Valesius in loc.

18. Psalm 131:7.

19. Literally, beneath the earth. *Note to the 2009 edition:* Though not mentioned in Scripture, the tradition that the stable of Christ's Nativity was actually a cave in Bethlehem can be traced back as far as Justin Martyr in the mid-Second century (see Catholic Encyclopedia, 1913 edition, *Nativity*).

20. Alluding, probably, to the discourse in Matthew 24, delivered by Our Lord to the disciples on the Mount of Olives.

21. These words seem to savor of Origen's doctrine, to which Eusebius was much addicted. Origen believed that, in the resurrection, bodies would be changed into souls, and souls into angels, according to the testimony of Jerome.

22. *Note to the 2009 edition:* Zosimus, writing nearly 200 years after the fact, claims that Constantine erected two pagan temples in Byzantium, placing a statue of the goddess Rhea in one and a statue of the Fortune of Rome in the other (*New History*, p. 53). But in the same passage, he also derides Constantine as someone contemptuous of (pagan) religion. Eusebius explains Constantine's placement of pagan statues in Constantinople in Book III, Chapter XLIII, pp. 139–141 of the present volume by asserting that he dragged them out of temples and into the light as a means of rebuking pagan superstitions and exposing them to ridicule.

23. Nicomedia, where Constantine had besieged Licinius, and compelled him to surrender, in memory of which event he built this church.

24. The English version in this passage (Genesis 18:1), and others, has "plains," though the Septuagint and ancient interpreters generally render it, as here, by "oak," some by "terebinth," (turpentine tree,) the Vulgate by "convallis."

25. Eutropia, mother of his empress Fausta.

26. On the coast of Cilicia, near Issus.

27. By Jupiter, for restoring Hippolytus to life, at Diana's request.

28. *Note to the 2009 edition:* Eusebius here refers to St. Paul, Philippians 1:18.

29. Eustathius, bishop of Antioch, whose deposition, on the ground of a charge of immorality, by the partisans of Eusebius of Nicomedia, had occasioned the disturbances alluded to in the text.

30. Alluding to the deposition of Eustathius, who had been charged with the crime of seduction. The reader who consults the original of this chapter, especially the latter part of it, may judge the difficulty of eliciting tolerable sense from an obscure and possibly corrupted text.

31. George (afterwards bishop of Laodicea) appears to have been degraded from the office of presbyter on the ground of impiety, by the same bishop who had ordained him. Both George and Euphronius were of the Arian party, of which fact it is possible that Constantine was ignorant.
32. Matthew 7:15, 16.

BOOK IV

CHAPTER I

CONSTANTINE CONFERS NUMEROUS HONORS IN THE WAY OF PRESENTS AND PROMOTIONS.

While thus variously engaged in promoting the extension and glory of the Church of God, and striving by every measure to commend the Savior's doctrine, the emperor was far from neglecting secular affairs, but in this respect also he was unwearied in bestowing benefits of every kind and in quick succession on the people of every province. On the one hand he manifested a paternal anxiety for the general welfare of his subjects, on the other he would distinguish individuals of his own acquaintance with various marks of honor, conferring his benefits in every instance in a truly noble spirit. No one could request a favor from the emperor and fail of obtaining what he sought. No one expected a boon from him, and found that expectation vain. Some received presents in money, others in land. Some obtained the Prætorian prefecture, others senatorial, others again consular rank. Many were appointed provincial governors. Others were made counts of the first, second, or third order. In numberless instances the title of Most Illustrious, and many other distinctions were conferred, for the emperor devised new dignitaries, that he might invest a larger number with the tokens of his favor.

CHAPTER II
REMISSION OF A FOURTH PART OF THE TRIBUTES.

The extent to which he studied the general happiness and prosperity may be understood from a single instance, most beneficial and universal in its application, and still gratefully remembered. He remitted a fourth part of the yearly tribute paid for land, and bestowed it on the owners of the soil, so that if we compute this yearly reduction, we shall find that the cultivators enjoyed their produce free of tribute every fourth year. This privilege being established by law, and secured for the time to come, has given occasion for the emperor's beneficence to be held, not merely by the then present generation, but by their children and descendants, in perpetual remembrance.

CHAPTER III
EQUALIZATION OF THE MORE OPPRESSIVE TAXES.

And whereas some persons found fault with the surveys of land which had been made under former emperors, and complained that their property was unduly burdened, acting in this case also on the principles of justice, he sent commissioners to equalize the tribute, and to secure indemnity to those who had made this appeal.

CHAPTER IV
HIS LIBERALITY, FROM HIS PRIVATE RESOURCES, TO THE LOSERS IN SUITS OF A PECUNIARY NATURE.

In cases of judicial arbitration, in order that the loser by his decision might not quit his presence less contented than the victorious litigant, he himself bestowed, and from his own private means, in some cases lands, in others money, on the defeated party. In this manner he took care that the loser, as having appeared in his presence, should be as well satisfied as the gainer of the cause. For he considered that no one ought in any case to retire dejected and sorrowful from an interview with such a prince. Thus it happened that both parties returned from the scene of trial with glad and cheerful countenances, while the emperor's noble-minded liberality excited universal admiration.

CHAPTER V

DEFEAT AND CONQUEST OF THE SCYTHIANS THROUGH THE STANDARD OF THE SAVIOR'S CROSS.

And why should I relate even briefly and incidentally, how he subjected barbarous nations to the Roman power, how he was the first who subjugated the Scythian[1] and Sarmatian tribes, which had never learned submission, and compelled them, how unwilling soever, to own the sovereignty of Rome? For the emperors who preceded him had actually rendered tribute to the Scythians, and Romans, by an annual payment, had confessed themselves servants to barbarians— an indignity which our emperor could no longer bear, nor think it consistent with his victorious career to continue the payment his predecessors had made. Accordingly, with full confidence in his Savior's aid, he raised his conquering standard against these enemies also, and soon reduced them all to obedience, coercing by military force those who fiercely resisted his authority, while, on the other hand, he conciliated the rest by wisely conducted embassies, and reclaimed them to a state of order and civilization from their lawless and savage life. Thus the Scythians at length learned to acknowledge subjection to the power of Rome.

CHAPTER VI
CONQUEST OF THE SARMATIANS, CONSEQUENT ON THE REBELLION OF THEIR SLAVES.

With respect to the Sarmatians, God Himself brought them beneath the rule of Constantine, and subdued a nation swelling with barbaric pride in the following manner. Being attacked by the Scythians, they had entrusted their slaves with arms, in order to repel the enemy. These slaves first overcame the invaders, and then, turning their weapons against their masters, drove them all from their native land. The expelled Sarmatians found that their only hope of safety was in Constantine's protection, and he, whose familiar habit it was to save men's lives, received them all within the confines of the Roman empire. Those who were capable of serving, he incorporated with his own troops. To the rest he allotted lands to cultivate for their own support, so that they themselves acknowledged that their past misfortune had produced a happy result, in that they now enjoyed Roman liberty in the place of savage barbarism. In this manner God added to his dominions many and various barbaric tribes.

CHAPTER VII
AMBASSADORS FROM DIFFERENT BARBAROUS NATIONS RECEIVE PRESENTS FROM THE EMPEROR.

Indeed, ambassadors were continually arriving from all nations, bringing for his acceptance their most precious gifts. So that I myself have sometimes stood near the entrance of the imperial palace, and observed a conspicuous array of barbarians in attendance, differing from each other in costume and decorations, and equally unlike in the fashion of their hair and beard. Their aspect truculent and terrible, their bodily stature prodigious. Some of a red complexion, others white as snow, others again of an intermediate color. For in the number of those I have referred to might be seen specimens of the Blemmyan tribes, of the Indians, and the Ethiopians,[2] "that widely divided race, remotest of mankind." All these in due succession (like some painted pageant), presented to the emperor those gifts which their own nation held in most esteem: some offering crowns of gold, others diadems set with precious stones, some bringing fair-haired boys, others barbaric vestments embroidered with gold and flowers. Some appeared with horses, others with shields and long spears, with arrows and bows, thereby offering their services and alliance for the emperor's acceptance. These presents he separately received and carefully laid aside, acknowledging them in so munificent a manner as at once to enrich those who bore them. He also honored the noblest among them with Roman offices of dignity, so that many of them thenceforward preferred to continue their residence among us, and felt no desire to revisit their native land.

CHAPTER VIII

HE WRITES TO THE KING OF PERSIA, WHO HAD SENT HIM AN EMBASSY, ON BEHALF OF THE CHRISTIANS IN HIS REALM.

The king of the Persians also having testified a desire to form an alliance with Constantine, by sending an embassy and presents as assurances of peace and friendship, the emperor in negotiating this treaty, far surpassed the monarch who had first done him honor in the magnificence with which he acknowledged his gifts. Having heard, too, that there were many churches of God in Persia, and that large numbers there were gathered into the fold of Christ, full of joy at this intelligence, he resolved to extend his anxiety for the general welfare to that country also, as one whose aim it was to care for all alike in every nation.

CHAPTER IX

LETTER OF CONSTANTINE AUGUSTUS TO SAPOR KING OF THE PERSIANS, CONTAINING A TRULY PIOUS CONFESSION OF GOD AND CHRIST.[3]

By keeping the Divine faith, I am made a partaker of the light of truth—guided by the light of truth, I advance in the knowledge of the Divine faith. Hence it is that (as my actions themselves evince), I profess the most holy religion. And this worship I declare to be that which teaches me deeper acquaintance with the most holy God, aided by whose Divine power, beginning from the very borders of the ocean, I have aroused each nation of the world in succession to a well-grounded hope of security, so that those which, groaning in servitude to the most cruel tyrants, and yielding to the pressure of their daily sufferings, had well nigh been utterly destroyed, have been restored through my agency to a far happier state.

This God I confess that I hold in unceasing honor and remembrance. This God I delight to contemplate with pure and guileless thoughts in the height of His glory. This God I invoke with bended knees, and recoil with horror from the blood of sacrifices, from their foul and detestable odors, and from every earth-born magic fire.[4] For the profane and impious superstitions which are defiled by these rites have cast down and consigned to perdition many, nay, whole nations of the Gentile world. For He who is Lord of all cannot endure that those blessings which, in His own loving kindness and consideration of the wants of men, He has revealed for the use of all, should be perverted to serve the lusts of any. His only demand from man is purity of mind and an undefiled spirit, and by this standard He weighs the actions of virtue and godliness. For His pleasure is in works of moderation and gentleness. He loves the meek, and hates the turbulent spirit. Delighting in faith, He chastises unbelief. By Him all presumptuous power is broken down, and He avenges the insolence of the proud. While the arrogant and haughty are utterly overthrown, He requites the humble and forgiving with deserved rewards. Even so does He highly honor and strengthen with His special help a kingdom justly governed, and maintains a prudent king in the tranquility of peace.

I cannot, then, my brother, believe that I err in acknowledging this one God, the author and parent of all things, whom many of my predecessors in power, led astray by the madness of error, have ventured to deny, but, who were all visited with a retribution so terrible and so destructive, that all succeeding generations have held up their calamities as the most effectual warning to any who desire to follow in their steps. Of the number of these I believe him[5] to have been, whom the lightning-stroke of Divine vengeance drove forth from hence, and banished to your dominions, and whose disgrace contributed to the fame of your much boasted triumph.

And it is surely a happy circumstance that the punishment of such persons as I have described should have been publicly manifested in our own times. For I myself have witnessed the end of those who lately harassed the worshippers of God by their impious edicts. And for this abundant thanksgivings are due to Him through whose excellent Providence all who observe His holy laws are gladdened by the renewed enjoyment of peace. Hence I am fully persuaded that everything is in the best and safest posture, since God is vouchsafing, through the influence of their pure and faithful religious service, and their unity of judgment respecting His Divine character, to gather all men to Himself.

Imagine, then, with what joy I heard tidings so accordant with my desire, that the fairest districts of Persia are to a great extent honored by the presence of that class of men on whose behalf alone I am at present speaking, I mean the Christians. I pray, therefore, that both you and they may enjoy abundant prosperity, and that your blessings and theirs may be in equal measure.[6] For thus you will experience the mercy and favor of that God who is the Lord and Father of all. And now, because your power is great, I commend these persons to your protection. Because your piety is eminent, I commit them to your care. Cherish them with your wonted humanity and kindness—for by this proof of faith you will secure an immeasurable benefit both to yourself and us.

CHAPTER X

HOW THE ZEALOUS PRAYERS OF CONSTANTINE PROCURED PEACE TO THE CHRISTIANS.

Thus, the nations of the world being everywhere guided in their course as it were by the skill of a single pilot, and acquiescing in the administration of him who governed as the servant of God, the peace of the Roman Empire continued undisturbed, and all classes of his subjects enjoyed a life of tranquility and repose. At the same time the emperor, who was convinced that the prayers of godly men contributed powerfully to the maintenance of the public welfare, felt himself constrained zealously to seek such prayers, and not only himself implored the help and favor of God, but charged the prelates of the churches to offer supplications on his behalf.

CHAPTER XI

HE CAUSES HIMSELF TO BE REPRESENTED ON HIS COINS, AND IN HIS PORTRAITS, IN THE ATTITUDE OF PRAYER.

How deeply his soul was impressed by the power of divine faith may be understood from the circumstance that he directed his likeness to be stamped on the golden coin of the empire with the eyes uplifted as in the posture of prayer to God. And this money became current throughout the Roman world. His portrait also at full length was placed over the entrance gates of the palaces in some cities, the eyes upraised to heaven, and the hands outspread as if in prayer.

CHAPTER XII

HE FORBIDS BY LAW THE PLACING OF HIS LIKENESS IN IDOL TEMPLES.

In this manner he represented himself, even through the medium of painting, as habitually engaged in prayer to God. At the same time he forbade, by an express enactment, the setting up of any resemblance of himself in any idol temple, that not even the mere lineaments of his person might receive contamination from the error of forbidden superstition.

CHAPTER XIII

OF HIS PRAYERS IN THE PALACE, AND HIS READING THE HOLY SCRIPTURES.

Still nobler proofs of his piety might be discerned by those who marked how he modeled as it were his very palace into a Church of God, and himself afforded a pattern of zeal to those assembled therein; how he took the sacred scriptures into his hands, and devoted himself to the study of those divinely inspired oracles, after which he would offer up regular prayers with all the members of his imperial court.

CHAPTER XIV

HE ENJOINS THE GENERAL OBSERVANCE OF THE LORD'S DAY, AND THE DAY BEFORE THE SABBATH.

He ordained, too, that one day should be regarded as a special occasion for prayer—I mean that which is truly the first and chief of all, the day of our Lord and Savior. The entire care of his household was entrusted to deacons and other ministers consecrated to the service of God, and distinguished by gravity of life and every other virtue, while his trusty body guard, strong in affection and fidelity to his person, found in their emperor an instructor in the practice of piety, and like him held the Lord's salutary day in honor, and performed on that day the devotions which he loved. The same observance was recommended by this blessed prince to all classes of his subjects, his earnest desire being gradually to lead all mankind to the worship of God. Accordingly he enjoined on all the subjects of the Roman empire to observe the Lord's day as a day of rest, and also to honor the day which precedes the sabbath, in memory, I suppose, of what the Savior of mankind is recorded to have achieved on that day.[7] And since his desire was to teach his whole army zealously to honor the Savior's day (which derives its name from light, and from the sun),[8] he freely granted to those among them who were partakers of the divine faith, leisure for attendance on the services of the Church of God, in order that they might be able, without impediment, to perform their religious worship.

CHAPTER XV

HE DIRECTED EVEN HIS PAGAN SOLDIERS TO PRAY ON THE LORD'S DAY.

With regard to those who were as yet ignorant of divine truth, he provided by a second statute that they should appear on each Lord's day on an plain near the city, and there, at a given signal, offer to God with one accord a prayer which they had previously learnt. He admonished them that confidence should not rest in their spears, or armor or bodily strength, but that they should acknowledge the supreme God as the giver of every good, and of victory itself, to whom they were bound to offer their prayers with due regularity, uplifting their hands toward heaven, and raising their mental vision higher still to the King of heaven, on whom they should call as the Author of victory, their Preserver, Guardian, and Helper. The emperor himself prescribed the prayer to be used by all his troops, commanding them to pronounce the following words in the Latin tongue.

CHAPTER XVI

THE FORM OF PRAYER GIVEN BY CONSTANTINE TO HIS SOLDIERS.

We acknowledge Thee the only God. We own Thee as our King, and implore Thy succor. By Thy favor have we gotten the victory. Through Thee are we mightier than our enemies. We render thanks for Thy past benefits, and trust Thee for future blessings. Together we pray to Thee, and beseech Thee long to preserve to us, safe and triumphant, our emperor Constantine and his pious sons.

Such was the duty to be performed on Sunday by his troops, and such the prayer they were instructed to offer up to God.

CHAPTER XVII

HE ORDERS THE SIGN OF THE CROSS TO BE ENGRAVEN ON HIS SOLDIERS' SHIELDS.

And not only so, but he also caused the sign of the salutary trophy to be impressed on the very shields of his soldiers, and commanded that his embattled forces should be preceded in their march, not by golden images, as heretofore, but only by the standard of the cross.

CHAPTER XVIII

OF HIS ZEAL IN PRAYER, AND THE HONOR HE PAID TO THE FEAST OF EASTER

The emperor himself, as a sharer in the holy mysteries of our religion, would seclude himself daily at a stated hour in the innermost chambers of his palace. And there, in solitary converse with his God, would kneel in humble supplication, and entreat the blessings of which he stood in need. But especially at the salutary feast of Easter, his religious diligence was redoubled. He fulfilled as it were the duties of a hierophant with every energy of his mind and body, and outvied all others in the zealous celebration of this feast. He changed, too, the holy night vigil into a brightness like that of day, by causing waxen tapers of great length to be lighted throughout the city besides which, torches every where diffused their light, so as to impart to this mystic vigil a brilliant splendor beyond that of day. As soon as day itself returned, in imitation of our Savior's gracious acts, he opened a liberal hand to his subjects of every nation, province, and people, and lavished abundant bounties on all.

CHAPTER XIX

HE FORBIDS IDOLATROUS WORSHIP, BUT HONORS MARTYRS AND THEIR FESTIVALS.

Such were his sacred ministrations in the service of his God. At the same time, his subjects, both civil and military, throughout the empire, found a barrier everywhere opposed against idol worship, and every kind of sacrifice forbidden.[9] A statute was also passed, enjoining the due observance of the Lord's day, and transmitted to the governors of every province, who undertook, at his command, to respect the days commemorative of martyrs, and duly to honor the festivals of the Church. And all these intentions were fulfilled to the emperor's entire satisfaction.

CHAPTER XX
HE DESCRIBES HIMSELF AS A BISHOP, IN CHARGE OF AFFAIRS EXTERNAL TO THE CHURCH.

Hence it was not without reason that once, on the occasion of his entertaining a company of bishops, he let fall the expression, "that he himself too was a bishop," addressing them in my hearing in the following words: "You are bishops whose jurisdiction is within the Church: I also am a bishop, ordained by God to overlook whatever is external to the Church." And truly his measures corresponded with his words, for he watched over his subjects with an episcopal care, and exhorted them as far as in him lay to follow a godly life.

CHAPTER XXI
PROHIBITION OF SACRIFICES, OF PROFANE MYSTERIES, AND COMBATS OF GLADIATORS: ALSO SUPPRESSION OF THE IMPIOUS PRIESTHOOD OF THE NILE.

Consistently with this zeal he issued successive laws and ordinances, forbidding any to offer sacrifice to idols, to consult diviners, to erect images, or to pollute the cities with the sanguinary combats of gladiators. And inasmuch as the Egyptians, especially those of Alexandria, had been accustomed to honor their river through a priesthood composed of effeminate men, a further law was passed commanding the extermination of these as a corrupt and vicious class of persons, that no one might thenceforward be found tainted with the like impurity. And whereas the superstitious inhabitants apprehended that the river would in consequence withhold its customary flood, God Himself

showed His approval of the emperor's law by ordering all
things in a manner quite contrary to their expectation. For
those who had defiled the cities by their vicious conduct
were indeed seen no more, but the river, as if the country
through which it flowed had been purified to receive it,
rose higher than ever before, and completely overflowed
the country with its fertilizing streams, thus effectually
admonishing the deluded people to turn from the impure
with abhorrence, and ascribe their prosperity to Him alone
who is the Giver of all good.

CHAPTER XXII

AMENDMENT OF THE LAW IN FORCE
RESPECTING CHILDLESS PERSONS,
AND OF THE LAW OF WILLS.

So numerous, indeed, were the benefits of this kind conferred
by the emperor on every province, as to afford ample materials
to any who might desire to record them. Among these may
be instanced those laws which he entirely remodeled, and
established on a more equitable basis, the nature of which
reform may be briefly and easily explained. The childless
were punished under the old law with the forfeiture of their
hereditary property. This merciless statute—which dealt
with persons thus circumstanced as positive criminals—
the emperor annulled, and regulated this question on the
principles of equity and justice. Willful transgressors, he
argued, should be chastised with the penalties their crimes
deserve. But nature herself denies children to many who
long, perhaps, for a numerous offspring, but are disappointed
of their hope by bodily infirmity. Others continue childless,
not from any dislike of posterity, but because their ardent
love of philosophy[10] renders them averse to the conjugal
union. Women, too, consecrated to the service of God, have

maintained a pure and spotless virginity, and have devoted themselves, soul and body, to a life of entire chastity and holiness. What then? Should this conduct be deemed worthy of punishment, or rather of admiration and praise, since to desire this state is in itself honorable, and to maintain it surpasses the power of unassisted nature? Surely those whose bodily infirmity destroys their hope of offspring are worthy of pity, not of punishment. And he who devotes himself to a higher object calls not for chastisement but especial admiration. On such principles of sound reason did the emperor rectify the defects of this law.

Again, with regard to the wills of dying persons, the old laws had ordained that they should be expressed, even at the latest breath, as it were, in certain definite words, and had prescribed the exact form and terms to be employed. This practice had occasioned many fraudulent attempts to hinder the intentions of the deceased from being carried into full effect. As soon as our emperor was aware of these abuses, he reformed this law likewise, declaring that a dying man ought to be permitted to indicate his last wishes in as few words as possible and in whatever terms he pleased, and to set forth his will in any written form, or even by word of mouth, provided it were done in the presence of proper witnesses who might be competent faithfully to discharge their trust.

CHAPTER XXIII

AMONG OTHER ENACTMENTS, HE FORBIDS THE JEWS TO POSSESS CHRISTIAN SLAVES, AND AFFIRMS THE VALIDITY OF THE DECISIONS OF COUNCILS.

He also passed a law to the effect, that no Christian should remain in servitude to a Jewish master, on the ground that it could not be right that those whom the Savior had ransomed should be subjected to the yoke of slavery by a people who had slain the prophets and the Lord Himself. If any were found hereafter in these circumstances, the slave was to be set at liberty, and the master punished by a fine.

He likewise added the sanction of his authority to the decisions of bishops passed at their synods, and forbade the provincial governors to rescind any of their decrees, for he rated the priests of God at a higher value than any judge whatever. These and a thousand similar provisions did he enact for the benefit of his subjects, but to give a special description of them, such as might convey an accurate idea of his imperial wisdom in these respects, would be a work of some time. Nor need I now relate at length, how, as a devoted servant of the Supreme God, he employed himself throughout the day in seeking objects for his beneficence, and how equally and universally kind he was to all.

CHAPTER XXIV

HIS OFFERINGS TO THE CHURCHES, AND DISTRIBUTIONS OF MONEY TO THE VIRGINS, AND TO THE POOR.

His liberality, however, was most especially exercised on behalf of the churches of God. In some cases he granted lands, in others he issued supplies of food for the support of the poor, of orphan children, and widows, besides which he evinced much care and forethought in fully providing the naked and destitute with clothing. He distinguished, however, with most special honor those who had devoted their lives to the practice of Divine philosophy. Hence his respect, little short of veneration, for God's most holy and ever virgin quire, for he felt assured that the God to whom such persons devoted themselves was Himself an inmate of their souls.

CHAPTER XXV

OF CONSTANTINE'S DISCOURSES AND DECLAMATIONS.

For himself, he sometimes passed sleepless nights in furnishing his mind with Divine knowledge, and much of his time was spent in composing discourses, many of which he delivered in public. For he conceived it to be incumbent on him to govern his subjects by appealing to their reason, and to secure in all respects a rational obedience to his authority. Hence he would sometimes himself convoke an assembly, on which occasions vast multitudes attended, in the hope of hearing an emperor sustain the part of a philosopher. And if in the course of his speech any occasion offered of touching on sacred topics, he immediately stood erect, and with a grave aspect and subdued tone of voice seemed reverently to be initiating his auditors in the mysteries of the Divine doctrine. And when they greeted him with shouts of acclamation, he would direct them by his gestures to raise their eyes to heaven, and reserve their admiration for the Supreme King alone, and honor Him with adoration and praise.

He usually divided the subjects of his address, first thoroughly exposing the error of polytheism, and proving the superstition of the Gentiles to be mere fraud, and a cloak for impiety. He then would assert the sole sovereignty of God; passing thence to His Providence, both general and particular. Proceeding next to the dispensation of salvation, he would demonstrate its necessity, and adaptation to the nature of the case, entering next in order on the doctrine of the Divine judgment. And here especially he appealed most powerfully to the consciences of his hearers, while he denounced the rapacious and violent, and those who were slaves to an inordinate thirst of gain. Nay, he caused some of his own acquaintance who were present to feel the severe lash of his words, and to stand with downcast eyes in the consciousness of guilt, while he testified against them in the clearest and most impressive terms that they would have an account to render of their deeds to God. He reminded them that God Himself had given him the empire of the world, portions of which he himself, acting on the same Divine principle, had entrusted to their government, but that all would in due time be alike summoned to give account of their actions to the Supreme Sovereign of all. Such was his constant testimony; such the subjects of his admonition and instruction. And he himself both felt and uttered these sentiments in the genuine confidence of faith. But his hearers were little disposed to learn, and deaf to sound advice; receiving his words indeed with loud applause, but induced by insatiable cupidity practically to disregard them.

CHAPTER XXVI

HE ATTEMPTS TO SHAME A COVETOUS PERSON, BY MARKING OUT BEFORE HIM THE MEASURE OF A GRAVE.

On one occasion he thus personally addressed one of his courtiers: "How far, my friend, are we to carry our inordinate desires?" Then drawing the dimensions of a human figure with a lance which he happened to have in his hand, he continued: "Though thou couldst obtain the whole wealth of this world, yea, the whole world itself, thou wilt carry with thee at last no more than this little spot which I have marked out, if indeed even that be thine."[11] Such were the words and actions of this blessed prince, and though at the time he failed to reclaim any from their evil ways, yet notwithstanding the course of events afforded evident proof that his admonitions rather resembled the Divine oracles than mere ordinary words.

CHAPTER XXVII

HE IS DERIDED BECAUSE OF HIS EXCESSIVE CLEMENCY.

Meantime, since there was no fear of capital punishment to deter from the commission of crime, for the emperor himself was uniformly inclined to clemency, and none of the provincial governors visited offences with their proper penalties, this state of things drew with it no small degree of blame on the general administration of the empire—whether justly or not, let every one form his own judgment—for myself, I only ask permission to record the fact.

CHAPTER XXVIII

OF CONSTANTINE'S ORATION WHICH HE WROTE TO THE ASSEMBLY OF THE SAINTS.

The emperor was in the habit of composing his orations in the Latin tongue, from which they were translated into Greek by interpreters appointed for this special service. One of the discourses thus translated I intend to annex, by way of specimen, to this present work (that one, I mean, which he inscribed to the assembly of the saints, and dedicated to the Church of God), that no one may have ground for deeming my testimony on this head mere empty praise.[12]

CHAPTER XXIX

HE LISTENED IN A STANDING POSTURE TO EUSEBIUS'S DECLAMATION IN HONOR OF OUR SAVIOR'S SEPULCHER.

One act, however, I must by no means omit to record, which this admirable prince performed in my own presence. On one occasion, emboldened by the confident assurance I entertained of his piety, I had begged permission to pronounce a discourse on the subject of our Savior's sepulcher in his hearing. With this request he most readily complied, and in the midst of a large number of auditors in the interior of the palace itself, he stood and listened with the rest. I entreated him (but in vain) to seat himself on the imperial throne which stood near: he continued with fixed attention to weigh the topics of my discourse, and gave his own testimony to the truth of the theological doctrines it contained. After some time had passed, the oration being of considerable length, I was myself desirous of concluding, but this he would not permit, and exhorted me to proceed to the very end. On my again entreating him to sit, he in his turn admonished me to desist, saying that it was not right to listen in a careless manner to the discussion of doctrines relating to God, and again, that this posture was good and profitable to himself, since it argued a becoming reverence to stand while listening to sacred truths. Having, therefore, concluded my discourse, I returned home, and resumed my usual occupations.

CHAPTER XXX
HE WRITES TO EUSEBIUS RESPECTING EASTER, AND THE SACRED BOOKS OF SCRIPTURE.

Ever careful for the welfare of the churches of God, the emperor addressed me personally in a letter on the means of providing copies of the inspired oracles, and also on the subject of the most holy feast of Easter. For I had myself dedicated to him an exposition of the mystical import of that feast, and the manner in which he honored me with a reply may be understood by any one who reads the following letter.

CHAPTER XXXI
CONSTANTINE'S LETTER TO EUSEBIUS, IN PRAISE OF HIS DISCOURSE CONCERNING EASTER.

Victor Constantinus, Maximus Augustus, to Eusebius.

It is indeed an arduous task, and beyond the power of language itself, worthily to treat of the mysteries of Christ, and to explain in a fitting manner the controversy respecting the feast of Easter, its origin as well as its precious and toilsome accomplishment.[13] For it is not in the power even of those who are able to apprehend them, adequately to describe the things of God. I am, notwithstanding, filled with admiration of your learning and zeal, and have not only myself read your work with pleasure, but have given directions, according to your own desire, that it be communicated to many sincere followers of our holy religion. Seeing, then, with what pleasure we receive favors of this kind from your Sagacity, be pleased to gladden us more frequently with those compositions, to the practice of which, indeed, you confess yourself to have been trained from an early period, so that I am urging a willing man (as they say), in exhorting you to your customary pursuits. And certainly the high and confident judgment we entertain is a proof that the person who has translated your writings into the Latin tongue is in no respect incompetent to the task, impossible though it be that such version should fully equal the excellence of the works themselves.

God preserve you, beloved brother.

Such was his letter on this subject, and that which related to the providing of copies of the scriptures for reading in the churches was to the following purport.

CHAPTER XXXII

CONSTANTINE'S LETTER TO EUSEBIUS ON THE PREPARATION OF COPIES OF THE SCRIPTURES.

Victor Constantinus, Maximus Augustus, to Eusebius.

It happens, through the favoring providence of God our Savior, that great numbers have united themselves to the most holy Church in the city which is called by my name. It seems, therefore, highly requisite, since that city is rapidly advancing in prosperity in all other respects, that the number of churches should also be increased. Do you, therefore, receive with all readiness my determination on this behalf. I have thought it expedient to instruct your Prudence to order fifty copies of the sacred scriptures (the provision and use of which you know to be most needful for the instruction of the Church) to be written on prepared parchment in a legible manner, and in a commodious and portable form, by transcribers thoroughly practiced in their art. The procurator of the diocese has also received instructions by letter from our Clemency to be careful to furnish all things necessary for the preparation of such copies, and it will be for you to take special care that they be completed with as little delay as possible.

You have authority also, in virtue of this letter, to use two of the public carriages for their conveyance, by which arrangement the copies when fairly written will most easily be forwarded for my personal inspection. And one of the deacons of your church may be entrusted with this service, who, on his arrival here, shall experience my liberality.

God preserve you, beloved brother!

CHAPTER XXXIII
HOW THE COPIES WERE PROVIDED.

Such were the emperor's commands, which were followed by the immediate execution of the work itself, which we sent him in magnificent and elaborate volumes of a threefold and fourfold form.[14] This fact is attested by another letter, which the emperor wrote in acknowledgment, in which, having heard that the city Constantia in our country, the inhabitants of which had been more than commonly devoted to superstition, had been impelled by a sense of religion to abandon their past idolatry, he testified his joy, and approval of their conduct.

CHAPTER XXXIV

THE PORT OF GAZA IS MADE A CITY FOR ITS PROFESSION OF CHRISTIANITY, AND RECEIVES THE NAME OF CONSTANTIA.

For in fact the place now called Constantia, in the province of Palestine, having embraced the saving religion, was distinguished both by the favor of God, and by special honor from the emperor, being now for the first time raised to the rank of a city, and receiving the more honored name of his pious sister in exchange for its former appellation.

CHAPTER XXXV

A PLACE IN PHŒNICIA ALSO IS MADE A CITY, AND IN OTHER CITIES IDOLATRY IS ABOLISHED, AND CHURCHES BUILT.

A similar change was effected in several other cities, for instance, in that town of Phœnicia which received its name, Constantina, from that of the emperor, and the inhabitants of which committed their innumerable idols to the flames, and adopted in their stead the principles of the saving faith. Numbers, too, in the other provinces, both in the cities and the country, became willing inquirers after the saving knowledge of God, destroyed as worthless things the images of every kind which they had heretofore held most sacred, voluntarily demolished the lofty temples and shrines which contained them, and, renouncing their former sentiments (or rather errors), commenced and completed entirely new churches. But since it is not so much my province to give a circumstantial detail of the actions of this pious prince, as it is theirs who have been privileged to enjoy his society at all times, I shall content myself with briefly recording such facts as have come to my own personal knowledge, before I proceed to notice the last days of his life.

CHAPTER XXXVI

HAVING CONFERRED THE DIGNITY OF CÆSARS ON HIS THREE SONS AT THE THREE DECENNIAL PERIODS OF HIS REIGN, HE DEDICATED THE CHURCH AT JERUSALEM.

By this time, the thirtieth year of his reign was completed. In the course of this period, his three sons had been admitted at different times as his colleagues in the empire.[15] The first, who bore his father's name, obtained this distinction about the tenth year of his reign. Constantius, the second son, so called from his grandfather, was proclaimed Cæsar about the twentieth, while Constans, the third (whose name expresses the firmness and stability of his character), was advanced to the same dignity at the thirtieth anniversary of his father's reign. Having thus reared a threefold offspring, a Trinity,[16] as it were, of pious sons, and having received them severally at each decennial period to a participation in his imperial authority, he judged the festival of his Tricennalia to be a fit occasion for thanksgiving to the Sovereign Lord of all, at the same time believing that the dedication of the church which his zealous magnificence had erected at Jerusalem might advantageously be performed.

CHAPTER XXXVII

IN THE MEANTIME HE ORDERS A COUNCIL TO BE CONVENED AT TYRE, BECAUSE OF CONTROVERSIES RAISED IN EGYPT.

Meanwhile that spirit of envy which is the enemy of all good, like a dark cloud intercepting the sun's brightest rays, endeavored to mar the joy of this festivity, by again raising contentions to disturb the tranquillity of the Egyptian churches. Our divinely favored emperor, however, once more convened a synod composed of many bishops, and set them as it were in armed array (like the host of God) against this malignant spirit, having commanded their presence from the whole of Egypt and Libya, from Asia, and from Europe, in order, first, to decide the questions in dispute, and afterwards to perform the dedication of the sacred edifice above mentioned. He enjoined them, by the way, to adjust their differences at the capital city of Phœnicia, reminding them that they had no right, while harboring feelings of mutual animosity, to engage in the service of God, since His law expressly forbids those who are at variance to offer their gift until they have first become reconciled and mutually disposed to peace.

Such were the salutary precepts which the emperor continually kept vividly before his own mind, and in accordance with which he admonished them to undertake their present duties in a spirit of perfect unanimity and concord, in a letter to the following purport.

CHAPTER XXXVIII

CONSTANTINE'S LETTER TO THE COUNCIL AT TYRE.

Victor Constantinus, Maximus Augustus, to the holy Council at Tyre.

Surely it would best consist with and best become the prosperity of these our times, that the Catholic Church should be undivided, and the servants of Christ be at this present moment clear from all reproach. Since, however, there are those who, carried away by a baleful and furious spirit of contention (for I will not charge them with intentionally leading a life unworthy of their profession), are endeavoring to create that general confusion which, in my judgment, is the most pernicious of all evils. I exhort you (forward as you already are) to meet together and form a synod without delay—to defend those who need protection, to administer remedies to your brethren who are in peril, to recall the divided members to unity of judgment, to rectify errors while opportunity is yet allowed—that, thus you may restore to so many provinces that due measure of concord which (strange and sad anomaly!) the arrogance of a few individuals has destroyed. And I believe that all are alike persuaded that this course is at the same time pleasing to Almighty God (as well as the highest object of my own desires), and will bring no small honor to yourselves, should you be successful in restoring peace. Delay not, then, but hasten with redoubled zeal to terminate the present dissensions in a manner becoming the occasion, by assembling together in that spirit of true sincerity and faith which the Savior whom we serve demands from us, I may almost say with an audible voice, on all occasions.

No proof of pious zeal on my part shall be wanting. Already have I done all to which my attention was directed by your letters. I have sent to those bishops whose presence you desired, that they may share your counsels. I have despatched Dionysius, a man of consular rank, who will both remind those prelates of their duty who are bound to attend the Council with you, and will himself be there to superintend the proceedings, but especially to maintain good order. Meantime should any one (though I deem it most improbable) venture on this occasion to violate my command, and refuse his attendance, a messenger shall be despatched forthwith to banish that person in virtue of an imperial edict, and to teach him that it does not become him to resist an emperor's decrees when issued in defense of truth. For the rest, it will be for your Holinesses, unbiased either by enmity or favor, but consistently with ecclesiastical and apostolic order, to devise a fitting remedy, whether it be for positive offenses or for unpremeditated errors, in order that, you may at once free the Church from all reproach, relieve my anxiety, and, by restoring the blessings of peace to those who are now divided, procure the highest honor for yourselves.

God preserve you, beloved brethren!

CHAPTER XXXIX

BISHOPS FROM EVERY PROVINCE ATTENDED THE DEDICATION OF THE CHURCH AT JERUSALEM.

No sooner had these injunctions been carried into effect, than another emissary arrived with dispatches from the emperor, and an urgent admonition to the Council to hasten their journey to Jerusalem without delay. Accordingly they all took their departure from the province of Phœnicia, and proceeded to their destination, availing themselves of the public means of transport. Thus Jerusalem became the gathering point for distinguished prelates from every province, and the whole city was thronged by a vast assemblage of the servants of God. The Macedonians had sent the bishop of their metropolis,[17] the Pannonians and Moesians the fairest of God's youthful flock among them.

A holy prelate from Persia too was there, deeply versed in the sacred oracles, while Bithynian and Thracian bishops graced the Council with their presence. Nor were the most illustrious from Cilicia wanting, nor the chief of the Cappadocians, distinguished above all for learning and eloquence. In short, the whole of Syria and Mesopotamia, Phœnicia and Arabia, Palestine, Egypt, and Libya, with the dwellers in the Thebaid, all contributed to swell the mighty concourse of God's ministers, followed as they were by vast numbers from every province, and each attended by an imperial escort. Officers of trust had also been sent from the palace itself, with instructions to heighten the splendor of the festival at the emperor's expense.

CHAPTER XL

OF THEIR RECEPTION BY THE NOTARY MACARIUS, THE DISTRIBUTION OF MONEY TO THE POOR, AND OFFERINGS TO THE CHURCH.

The director and chief of these officers was a most useful servant of the emperor, a man eminent for faith and piety, and thoroughly acquainted with the Divine word, who had been honorably conspicuous by his profession of godliness during the time of the tyrants' power, and therefore was deservedly entrusted with the arrangement of the present proceedings. Accordingly, in faithful obedience to the emperor's commands, he received the assembly with courteous hospitality, and entertained them with feasts and banquets on a scale of great splendor. He also distributed lavish supplies of money and clothing among the naked and destitute, and the multitudes of both sexes who suffered from want of food and the common necessaries of life. Finally, he enriched and beautified the church itself throughout with offerings of imperial magnificence, and thus fully accomplished the service he had been commissioned to perform.

CHAPTER XLI

VARIOUS DISCOURSES BY THE ASSEMBLED BISHOPS, ALSO BY EUSEBIUS THE WRITER OF THIS HISTORY.

Meantime, the festival derived additional luster both from the prayers and discourses of the ministers of God, some of whom extolled the pious emperor's willing devotion to the Savior of mankind, and dilated on the magnificence of the edifice which he had raised to His memory. Others afforded, as it were, an intellectual feast to the ears of all present, by public disquisitions on the sacred doctrines of our religion. Others interpreted passages of holy Scripture, and unfolded their hidden meaning, while such as were unequal to these efforts presented a bloodless sacrifice and mystical service to God in the prayers which they offered for general peace, for the Church of God, for the emperor himself as the instrumental cause of so many blessings, and for his pious sons. I myself too, unworthy as I was of such a privilege, pronounced various public orations in honor of this solemnity, wherein I partly explained by a written description the details of the imperial edifice, and partly endeavored to gather from the prophetic visions apt illustrations of the symbols it displayed.[18] Thus joyfully was the festival of dedication celebrated in the thirtieth year of our emperor's reign.

CHAPTER XLII
EUSEBIUS AFTERWARDS REPEATED HIS DESCRIPTION OF THE CHURCH, AND HIS ORATION ON THE TRICENNALIA, BEFORE CONSTANTINE HIMSELF.

The structure of the church of our Savior, the form of His sacred cave, the splendor and elegance of the work itself, and the numberless offerings in gold, and silver, and precious stones, I have described to the best of my ability, and dedicated to the emperor in a separate treatise, which on a fitting opportunity I shall append to this present work.[19] I shall add to it also that oration on his Tricennalia which shortly afterwards, having travelled to the city which bears his name, I delivered in the emperor's own presence. This was the second opportunity afforded me of glorifying the Supreme God in the imperial palace itself, and on this occasion my pious hearer evinced the greatest joy, as he afterwards testified, when he entertained the bishops then present, and loaded them with distinctions of every kind.

CHAPTER XLIII
THE COUNCIL AT NICAEA WAS HELD IN THE TWENTIETH, THE DEDICATION OF THE CHURCH AT JERUSALEM IN THE THIRTIETH YEAR OF CONSTANTINE'S REIGN.

This second synod the emperor convened at Jerusalem, being the greatest of which we have any knowledge, next to the first which he had summoned at the famous Bithynian city. That indeed was a triumphal assembly, held in the twentieth year of his reign, an occasion of thanksgiving for victory over his enemies in the very city which bears the name of victory. The present meeting added luster to the thirtieth anniversary, during which the emperor dedicated the church at the sepulcher of our Savior, as a peace-offering to God the Giver of all good.

CHAPTER XLIV

CONSTANTINE TESTIFIES HIS AVERSION TO EXCESSIVE PRAISE.

And now that all these ceremonies were completed, and the divine qualities of the emperor's character continued to be the theme of universal praise, one of God's ministers presumed so far as in his own presence to pronounce him blessed, as having been counted worthy to hold absolute and universal empire in this life, and as being destined to share the empire of the Son of God in the world to come. These words, however, Constantine heard with indignation, and forbade the speaker to hold such language, exhorting him rather to pray earnestly on his behalf, that whether in this life or in that which is to come, he might be found worthy to be a servant of God.

CHAPTER XLV

MARRIAGE OF HIS SON CONSTANTIUS CÆSAR

On the completion of the thirtieth year of his reign he solemnized the marriage of his second son, having concluded that of his first-born long before. This was an occasion of great joy and festivity, the emperor himself attending on his son at the ceremony, and entertaining the guests of both sexes (the men and women in distinct and separate companies) with sumptuous hospitality, Rich presents likewise were liberally distributed among the cities and people.

CHAPTER XLVI

AN EMBASSY ARRIVES, WITH PRESENTS, FROM THE INDIANS.

About this time ambassadors from the Indians, who inhabit the distant regions of the East, arrived with presents consisting of many varieties of brilliant precious stones, and animals differing in species from those known to us. These offerings they presented to the emperor, thus allowing that his sovereignty extended even to the Indian Ocean, and that the princes of their country, who rendered homage to him both by paintings and statues, acknowledged his imperial and paramount authority. Thus the Eastern Indians now submitted to his sway, as the Britons of the Western Ocean had done at the commencement of his reign.

CHAPTER XLVII

CONSTANTINE DIVIDES THE EMPIRE BETWEEN HIS THREE SONS, WHOM HE HAD INSTRUCTED IN THE ARTS OF GOVERNMENT AND THE DUTIES OF RELIGION.

Having thus established his power in the opposite extremities of the world, he divided the whole extent of his dominions, as though he were allotting a patrimonial inheritance to the dearest objects of his regard, among his three sons. To the eldest he assigned his grandfather's portion, to the second, the empire of the East, to the third, the countries which lie between these two divisions.[20] And being desirous of furnishing his children with an inheritance truly valuable and salutary to their souls, he had been careful to imbue them with true religious principles, being himself their guide to the knowledge of sacred things, and also appointing men

194

of approved piety to be their instructors. At the same time he assigned them the most accomplished teachers of secular learning, by some of whom they were taught the arts of war, while they were trained by others in political, and by others again in legal science. To each moreover was granted a truly royal retinue, consisting of infantry, spearmen, and body guards, with every other kind of military force, commanded respectively by captains, tribunes, and generals of whose warlike skill and devotion to his sons the emperor had had previous experience.

CHAPTER XLVIII

HIS PIOUS INSTRUCTIONS AFTER THEY HAD REACHED MATURITY.

As long as the Cæsars were of tender years, they were aided by suitable advisors in the management of public affairs, but on their arrival at the age of manhood their father's instructions alone sufficed. When present, he proposed to them his own example, and admonished them to follow his pious course. In their absence he furnished them by letter with rules of conduct suited to their imperial station, the first and greatest of which was an exhortation to value the knowledge and worship of the Sovereign Lord of all more than any wealth, nay, more than empire itself. At length he permitted them to direct the public administration of the empire without control, making it his first request that they would care for the interests of the Church of God, and boldly profess themselves disciples of Christ. Thus trained and excited to obedience not so much by precept as by their own voluntary desire for virtue, his sons more than fulfilled the admonitions of their father, devoting their earnest attention to the service of God, and observing the ordinances of the Church even in the palace itself, with all the members of their households. For their father's forethought had provided that all the attendants of his sons should be Christians. And not only so, but the military officers of highest rank, and those who had the control of public business, were professors of the same faith. For the emperor placed confidence in the fidelity of men devoted to the service of God, as in a strong and sure defense.

It was after our thrice blessed prince had completed these arrangements, and thus secured order and tranquility throughout the empire, that God, the Dispenser of all blessings, judged it to be the fitting time to translate him to a better inheritance, and summoned him to pay the debt of nature.

CHAPTER XLIX

HAVING REIGNED ABOUT THIRTY TWO YEARS, AND LIVED ABOVE SIXTY, HE STILL ENJOYED SOUND BODILY HEALTH.

He completed the time of his reign in two and thirty years, wanting a few months and days,[21] and his whole life extended to about twice that period. At this age he still possessed a sound and vigorous body, free from all blemish, and of more than youthful vivacity—a noble mien, and strength equal to any exertion—so that he was able to join in martial exercises, to ride, endure the fatigues of travel, engage in battle, and erect trophies over his conquered enemies, besides gaining those bloodless victories by which he was wont to triumph over those who opposed him.

CHAPTER L

HIS EXTREME BENEVOLENCE WAS ABUSED BY SOME AS AN ENCOURAGEMENT TO AVARICE AND HYPOCRISY.

In like manner his mental qualities reached the highest point of human perfection. Indeed he was distinguished by every excellence of character, but especially by benevolence—a virtue, however, which subjected him to censure from many, in consequence of the baseness of wicked men, who ascribed their own crimes to the emperor's forbearance. In truth I can myself bear testimony to the grievous evils which prevailed during these times: I mean the violence of rapacious and unprincipled men, who preyed on all classes of society alike, and the scandalous hypocrisy of those who crept into the Church, and assumed the name and character of Christians. His own benevolence and goodness of heart, the genuineness of his own faith, and his truthfulness of character, induced the emperor to credit the profession of these reputed Christians, who craftily preserved the semblance of sincere affection for his person. The confidence he reposed in such men sometimes forced him into conduct unworthy of himself, of which envy took advantage to cloud in this respect the luster of his character.

CHAPTER LI

CONSTANTINE EMPLOYED HIMSELF IN COMPOSITION OF VARIOUS KINDS TO THE CLOSE OF HIS LIFE.

These offenders, however, were soon overtaken by divine chastisement. To return to our emperor. He had so thoroughly trained his mind in the art of reasoning that he continued to the last to compose discourses on various subjects, to deliver frequent orations in public, and to instruct his hearers in the sacred doctrines of religion. He was also habitually engaged in legislating both on political and military questions—in short, in devising whatever might be conducive to the general welfare of the human race. It is well worthy of remark that very shortly before his departure, he pronounced a funeral oration before his usual auditory, in which he spoke at length on the immortality of the soul, the state of those who had persevered in a life of godliness, and the blessings which God has laid up in store for them that love Him.

On the other hand, he made it appear by copious and conclusive argument what the end of those will be who have pursued a contrary career, describing in vivid language the final ruin of the ungodly. His powerful testimony on these subjects seemed so far to touch the consciences of those around him, that one of the self-imagined philosophers, of whom he asked his opinion of what he had heard, bore testimony to the truth of his words, and accorded a real, though reluctant tribute of praise, to the arguments by which he had exposed the worship of a plurality of Gods. By converse such as this with his friends before his death, the emperor seemed as it were to smooth and prepare the way for his transition to a happier life.

CHAPTER LII

HE IS ATTENDED BY BISHOPS ON AN EXPEDITION AGAINST THE PERSIANS, AND TAKES WITH HIM A TENT IN THE FORM OF A CHURCH.

It is also worthy of record that about the time of which I am at present writing, the emperor, having heard of an insurrection of some barbarians in the East, observed that the conquest of this enemy was still in store for him, and resolved on an expedition against the Persians. Accordingly he proceeded at once to put, his forces in motion, at the same time communicating his intended march to the bishops who happened to be at his court, some of whom he judged it right to take with him as companions, and as needful coadjutors in the service of God. They, on the other hand, cheerfully declared their willingness to follow in his train, disclaiming any desire to leave him, and engaging to battle with and for him by supplication to God on his behalf. Full of joy at this answer to his request, he unfolded to them his projected line of march, after which he caused a tent of great splendor, representing in shape the figure of a church, to be prepared for his own use in the approaching war. In this he intended to unite with the bishops in offering prayers to the God from whom all victory proceeds.

CHAPTER LIII

HIS FAVORABLE RECEPTION OF AN EMBASSY FROM THE PERSIANS. HE KEEPS THE NIGHT VIGIL WITH OTHERS AT THE FEAST OF EASTER.

In the mean while the Persians, hearing of the Emperor's warlike preparations, and not a little terrified at the prospect of an engagement with his forces, dispatched an embassy to pray for conditions of peace. These overtures the emperor, himself a sincere lover of peace, at once accepted, and readily entered on friendly relations with that people. At this time, the great festival of Easter was at hand, on which occasion he rendered the tribute of his prayers to God, and passed the night in watching with the assembled worshippers.

CHAPTER LIV
BUILDING OF A CHURCH IN HONOR OF THE APOSTLES AT CONSTANTINOPLE.

After this he proceeded to erect a church in memory of the apostles in the city which bears his name. This building he carried to a vast height, and brilliantly decorated by encasing it from the foundation to the roof with marble slabs of various colors. He also formed the inner roof of finely fretted work, and overlaid it throughout with gold. The external covering, which protected the building from the weather, was of brass instead of tiles; and this too was splendidly and profusely adorned with gold, and reflected the sun's rays with a brilliancy which dazzled the distant beholder. The dome was entirely encompassed by a finely carved tracery, wrought in brass and gold.

CHAPTER LV
FURTHER DESCRIPTION OF THE SAME CHURCH.

Such was the magnificence with which the emperor was pleased to beautify this church. The building was surrounded by an open area of great extent, the four sides of which were terminated by porticos which enclosed the area and the church itself. Adjoining these porticos were ranges of stately chambers, with baths and lodging rooms, and many other apartments adapted to the use of those who had charge of the place.

CHAPTER LVI

HE ALSO ERECTED HIS OWN SEPULCHRAL MONUMENT IN THIS CHURCH.

All these edifices the emperor consecrated with the desire of perpetuating the memory of the apostles of our Savior. He had, however, another object in erecting this building—an object at first unknown, but which afterwards became evident to all. He had in fact made choice of this spot in the prospect of his own death, anticipating with extraordinary fervor of faith that his body would share their title with the apostles themselves, and that he should thus even after death become the subject, with them, of the devotions which should be performed to their honor in this place. He accordingly caused twelve coffins to be set up in this church, like sacred pillars in honor and memory of the apostolic number, in the centre of which his own was placed, having six of theirs on either side of it. Thus, as I said, he had provided with prudent foresight an honorable resting-place for his body after death, and having long before secretly formed this resolution, he now consecrated this church to the apostles, believing that this tribute to their memory would be of no small advantage to his own soul.

Nor did God disappoint him of that which he so ardently expected and desired. For after he had completed the first services of the feast of Easter, and had passed this sacred day of our Lord in a manner which made it an occasion of joy and gladness to himself and to all, the God through whose aid he performed all these acts, and whose zealous servant he continued to be even to the end of life, was pleased at a happy time to translate him to a higher and better sphere of being.

CHAPTER LVII

HIS SICKNESS AT HELENOPOLIS, AND PRAYERS RESPECTING HIS BAPTISM.

At first he experienced some slight interruption of his usual health, which was soon followed by positive disease. In consequence of this he visited the hot baths of his own city, and thence proceeded to that which bore the name of his mother. Here he passed some time in the church of the martyrs, and offered up supplications and prayers to God. Being at length convinced that his life was drawing to a close, he felt the time was come at which he should seek to expiate the errors of his past career, firmly believing that whatever sins he had committed as a mortal man, his soul would be purified from them through the efficacy of the mysterious words and the salutary waters of baptism. Impressed with these thoughts, he poured forth his supplications and confessions to God, kneeling on the pavement in the church itself, in which he also now for the first time received the imposition of hands with prayer.[22] After this he proceeded as far as the suburbs of Nicomedia, and there, having summoned the bishops to meet him, addressed them in the following words.

CHAPTER LVIII

CONSTANTINE'S APPEAL TO THE BISHOPS, REQUESTING THEM TO CONFER UPON HIM THE RITE OF BAPTISM.

The time is arrived which I have long hoped for, with an earnest desire and prayer that I might obtain the salvation of God. The hour is come in which I too may receive the blessing of that seal which confers immortality—the hour in which I may partake of the impression of the salutary sign. I had thought to do this in the waters of the river Jordan, wherein our Savior, for our example, is recorded to have been baptized. But God, who knows what is expedient for us, is pleased that I should receive this blessing here. Be it so, then, without delay. For should it be His will who is Lord of life and death, that my existence here should be prolonged, and should I be destined henceforth to associate with the people of God, and unite with them in prayer as a member of His Church, I will prescribe to myself from this time such a course of life as befits His service.

After he had thus spoken, the prelates performed the sacred ceremonies in the usual manner, and having given him the necessary instructions, made him a partaker of the mystic ordinance. Thus was Constantine the first of all sovereigns who was regenerated and perfected in a church dedicated to the martyrs of Christ. Thus gifted with the Divine seal of baptism, he rejoiced in spirit, was renewed, and filled with heavenly light. His soul was gladdened by reason of the fervency of his faith, and astonished at the manifestation of the power of God. At the conclusion of the ceremony he arrayed himself in imperial vestments, white and brilliant as the light,[23] and reclined on a couch of the purest white, refusing to clothe himself with the purple any more.

CHAPTER LIX
AFTER HIS BAPTISM HE RENDERS THANKS TO GOD.

He then lifted his voice and poured forth a strain of thanksgiving to God, after which he added these words: "Now I know that I am truly blessed. Now I feel assured that I am accounted worthy of immortality, and am made a partaker of Divine light."

He further expressed his compassion for the unhappy condition of those who were strangers to such blessings as he enjoyed. And when the tribunes and generals of his army appeared in his presence with lamentations and tears at the prospect of their bereavement, and with prayers that his days might yet be prolonged, he assured them in reply that he was now in possession of true life—that none but himself could know the value of the blessings he had received—so that he was anxious rather to hasten than to defer his departure to God. He then proceeded to complete the needful arrangement of his affairs, bequeathing an annual donation to the Roman inhabitants of his imperial city, apportioning the inheritance of his empire like a patrimonial estate among his own children; in short, making every other disposition according to his own judgment and desire.

CHAPTER LX
CONSTANTINE'S DEATH AT NOON ON THE FEAST OF PENTECOST.

All these events occurred during a most important festival, I mean the august and holy solemnity of Pentecost, which is distinguished by a period of seven weeks, and crowned with that one day on which the holy scriptures attest the reception of our common Savior into heaven, and the descent of the Holy Spirit, among men. In the course of this feast the emperor received the privileges I have described, and on the last day of all, which one might justly call the feast of feasts, he was removed about mid-day to the presence of his God, leaving his mortal remains to his fellow mortals, and carrying into fellowship with God that part of his being which was capable of understanding and loving Him. Such was the close of Constantine's mortal life. Let us now attend to the circumstances which followed this event.

CHAPTER LXI

LAMENTATIONS OF THE SOLDIERY AND THEIR OFFICERS.

Immediately the assembled spearmen and bodyguard rent their garments, and prostrated themselves on the ground, striking their heads, and uttering lamentations and cries of sorrow, calling on their imperial lord and master, or rather, like fond and affectionate children, on their father, while their tribunes and centurions addressed him as their preserver, protector, and benefactor. The rest of the soldiery also came in respectful order to mourn as a flock the removal of their good shepherd. The people meanwhile ran wildly throughout the city—some expressing the inward sorrow of their hearts by loud cries, others appearing confounded with grief—each mourning the event as a calamity which had befallen himself, and bewailing his death as though they felt themselves bereft of a blessing common alike to all.

CHAPTER LXII

REMOVAL OF THE BODY FROM NICOMEDIA TO THE PALACE AT CONSTANTINOPLE.

After this, the soldiers lifted the body from its couch, and laid it in a golden coffin, which they enveloped in a covering of purple, and removed to the city which was called by his own name. Here it was placed in an elevated position in the principal chamber of the imperial palace, and surrounded by candles burning in candlesticks of gold, presenting a marvellous spectacle, and such as no mortal had exhibited on earth, since the world itself began. For in the central apartment of the imperial palace, the body of the emperor lay in its elevated resting-place, arrayed in the symbols of sovereignty, the diadem and purple robe, and encircled by a numerous retinue of attendants, who watched around it incessantly night and day.

CHAPTER LXIII

HE RECEIVED THE SAME HONORS FROM THE COUNTS AND OTHER OFFICERS AS BEFORE HIS DEATH.

The military officers, too, of the highest rank, the counts, and the whole order of magistrates, who had been accustomed to do obeisance to their emperor before his death, continued to fulfill this duty without any change, entering the chamber at the appointed times, and saluting their coffined sovereign with bended knee, as though he were still alive. After them the senators appeared, and all who had been distinguished by any honorable office, and rendered the same homage. These were followed by multitudes of every rank, who came with their wives and children to witness the spectacle.

These honors continued to be rendered for a considerable time, the soldiers having resolved thus to guard the body until his sons should arrive, and take on themselves the conduct of their father's funeral. No mortal had ever, like this blessed prince, continued to reign even after death, and to receive the same homage as during his life. He only, of all who have ever lived, obtained this reward from God—a suitable reward, since he alone of all sovereigns had in all his actions honored the Supreme God and His Christ. And God Himself accordingly was pleased that even his mortal remains should still retain imperial authority among men, thus indicating to all who were not utterly devoid of understanding the immortal and endless empire which his soul was destined to enjoy.

CHAPTER LXIV.

RESOLUTION OF THE ARMY TO CONFER THENCE-FORWARD THE TITLE OF AUGUSTUS ON HIS SONS.

Meanwhile the tribunes selected from the troops under their command those officers whose fidelity and zeal had long been known to the emperor, and despatched them to the Cæsars with intelligence of the late event. This service they accordingly performed. As soon, however, as the soldiery throughout the provinces received the tidings of the emperor's decease, they all, as if by a supernatural impulse, resolved with one consent (as though their great emperor had been yet alive) to acknowledge none other than his sons as sovereigns of the Roman world. And these they soon after determined should no longer retain the name of Cæsar, but should each be honored with the title of Augustus, a name which indicates the highest supremacy of imperial power. Such were the measures adopted by the army, and these resolutions they communicated to each other by letter, so that the unanimous desire of the legions became known at the same point of time throughout the whole extent of the empire.

CHAPTER LXV

MOURNING FOR CONSTANTINE AT ROME, AND PAINTINGS IN MEMORY OF HIS DEATH.

On the arrival of the news of the emperor's death in the imperial city, the Roman senate and people felt the announcement as the heaviest and most afflictive of all calamities, and gave themselves up to an excess of grief. The baths and markets were closed, the public spectacles, and all other recreations in which men of leisure are accustomed to indulge, were interrupted. Those who had erewhile lived in luxurious ease, now walked the streets in gloomy sadness, while all united in blessing the name of the deceased, as the friend of heaven, and truly worthy of the imperial dignity. Nor was their sorrow expressed only in words—they proceeded also to honor him, by the dedication of paintings to his memory, with the same respect as before his death. The design of these pictures embodied a representation of heaven itself, and depicted the emperor reposing in an ethereal mansion above the celestial vault. They too declared his sons to be his only successors in the imperial power and the title of Augustus, and begged with earnest entreaty that they might be permitted to receive the body of their emperor, and perform his obsequies in the imperial city.

CHAPTER LXVI

HIS BURIAL BY HIS SON CONSTANTIUS AT CONSTANTINOPLE.

Thus did the citizens of Rome testify their respect for the memory of him who had been honored by God. The second of his sons, however, who had by this time arrived, proceeded to celebrate his father's funeral in the city which bears his name, himself heading the procession, which was preceded by detachments of soldiers in military array, and followed by vast multitudes, the body itself being surrounded by companies of spearmen and heavy-armed infantry. On the arrival of the procession at the church dedicated to the apostles of our Savior, the coffin was there entombed. Such honor did the youthful emperor Constantius render to his deceased parent, both by his presence, and by the due performance of this sacred ceremony.

CHAPTER LXVII

SACRED SERVICE IN THE CHURCH OF THE APOSTLES ON THE OCCASION OF CONSTANTINE'S FUNERAL.

As soon as Constantius had withdrawn himself with the military train, the ministers of God came forward with the multitude and the whole congregation of the faithful, and performed the rites of Divine worship with prayer. At the same time the tribute of their praises was given to the character of this blessed prince, whose body rested on a lofty and conspicuous monument, and the whole multitude united with the priests of God in offering prayers for his soul with many tears, thus performing an office consonant with the desires of the pious deceased.[24] In this respect also the favor of God was manifested to His servant in that he not only bequeathed the succession of the empire to his own beloved sons, but that the earthly tabernacle of his thrice blessed soul, according to his own earnest wish, was permitted to share the monument of the apostles, was associated with the honor of their name, and with that of the people of God, was honored by the performance of the sacred ordinances and mystic service; and enjoyed a participation in the prayers of the saints. Thus, too, he continued to possess imperial power even after death, controlling, as though with renovated life, a universal dominion, and retaining in his own name, as Victor Maximus Augustus, the sovereignty of the Roman world.[25]

CHAPTER LXVIII

AN ALLUSION TO THE PHOENIX.

We cannot compare him with that bird of Egypt—the only one, as they say, of its kind—which dies, self-sacrificed, in the midst of aromatic perfumes, and rising from its own ashes with new life, soars aloft in the same form which it had before. Rather did he resemble his Savior, who, as the sown corn which is multiplied from a single grain, had yielded abundant increase through the blessing of God, and had over-spread the world with His fruit. Even so did our thrice blessed prince become multiplied, as it were, through the succession of his sons. His statue was erected along with theirs in every province, and the name of Constantine was owned and honored even after the close of his mortal life.

CHAPTER LXIX

CONSTANTINE IS REPRESENTED ON COINS IN THE ACT OF ASCENDING TO HEAVEN.

A coinage was also struck which bore the following device. On one side appeared the figure of our blessed prince, with the head closely veiled, the reverse exhibited him sitting as a charioteer, drawn by four horses, with a hand stretched downward from above to receive him up to heaven.

CHAPTER LXX

THE GOD WHOM HE HAD HONORED DESERVEDLY HONORED HIM IN RETURN.

Such are the proofs by which the Supreme God has made it manifest to us, in the person of him who alone of all sovereigns had openly professed the Christian faith, how great a difference He perceives between those whose privilege it is to worship Him and His Christ, and those who have chosen the contrary part, who provoked His enmity by daring to assail His Church, and whose calamitous end, in every instance, afforded tokens of His displeasure, as manifestly as the death of Constantine conveyed to all men an evident assurance of His Divine love.

CHAPTER LXXI

HE SURPASSED ALL PRECEDING EMPERORS IN DEVOTION TO GOD.

Standing, as he did, alone and preeminent among the Roman emperors as a worshipper of God—alone as the bold proclaimer to all men of the doctrine of Christ, having alone rendered honor, as none before him had ever done, to

211

His Church, having alone abolished utterly the superstitious worship of a plurality of gods, and discountenanced idolatry in every form—so, both during life and after death, was he accounted worthy of such honors as none can say have been attained to by any other, so that no one, whether Greek or barbarian, nay, of the ancient Romans themselves, has ever been presented to us as worthy of comparison with him.

END OF THE LIFE OF CONSTANTINE.

NOTES

1. Probably the Goths are meant, as in Socrates's *Ecclesiastical History*, book i, chap. 18, p. 49.

2. Αἰθίοπας, τοὶ διχθὰ δεδαίαται ἔσχατοι ἀνδρῶν, Οἱ μὲν δυσομένου ὑπερίονος, οἱ δ᾽ ἀνιόντος. – Odyss. i. 23, 24.

3. *Note to the 2009 edition:* Superfluous chapter titles have again been omitted here. See Book II, note 10, p. 98 of the present volume.

4. This refers to the luminous appearances produced by the pagan priests in the celebration of their mysteries.

5. Valerian, who had been a persecutor of the Christians, and whose expedition against the Persians had terminated in his own captivity and subjection to every kind of insult and cruelty from the conquerors.

6. The sense given above of this passage (which in the text is corrupt), is founded on the reading restored by Valesius from Theodoritus and Nicephorus.

7. That is, Friday. The passage is not very intelligible. Does it mean that Constantine ordered this day to be distinguished in some way from others, as the day of the Lord's crucifixion?

8. The decree of Constantine for the general observance of Sunday appears to have been issued AD 321, before which time both "the old and new sabbath" were observed by Christians. "Constantine (says Gibbon, chap. xx, note 8) styles the Lord's day *Dies solis*, a name which could not offend the ears of his Pagan subjects."

9. This prohibition must be limited to private sacrifices. See Book II, note 15, p. 98.

10. The word "philosophy," here and in the 28th chapter, plainly indicates that virginity which was so highly honored in the earlier ages of Christianity.

11. Since it is uncertain whether thou wilt be buried in the ground, or consumed by fire, or drowned in the sea, or devoured by wild beasts.—Valesius in loc.

12. *Note to the 2009 edition:* Eusebius is referring here to the *Oration of Constantine to the Assembly of the Saints*, which may be found appended to the 1845 Bagster edition of *The Life of the Blessed Emperor Constantine.* It will be published as a separate volume in this present series along with *The Oration of Eusebius in Praise of the Emperor Constantine.*

13. i.e., through the sufferings and resurrection of Christ.

14. The parchment copies were usually arranged in quaternions, i.e., four leaves made up together, as the ternions consisted of three leaves. The quaternions each contained sixteen pages, the ternions twelve. Valesius in loc.

15. *Note to the 2009 edition:* In keeping with the adulatory tenor of his work, Eusebius neglects to mention Constantine's eldest son, Crispus, sired during his first marriage to Minervina. Crispus had also been Cæsar, but was executed by the command of his father based on accusations made by his step-mother, Fausta, Constantine's second wife. For reasons not altogether clear, Constantine also ordered Fausta executed shortly thereafter. For a good summary of this tragic episode, see Odahl, pp. 204–209.

16. Τριάδος λόγῳ. Well may the old English Translator remark on this, "An odd expression." We may go further, and denounce it as an instance of the senseless and profane adulation to which our author, perhaps in the spirit of his age, seems to have been but too much inclined.

17. Alexander, bishop of Thessalonica. By the Pannonian and Moesian bishops are meant Ursacius and Valens, leaders of the Arian party, by the Bithynian and Thracian, Theogonius of Nicaea, and Theodorus of Perinthus. —Valesius.

18. Eusebius gives us no example of his application of Scripture in this case. His commentator Valesius refers to Zephaniah 3:8 (LXX.), Διὰ τοῦτο ὑπόμεινόν με, λέγει Κύριος, εἰς ἡμέραν ἀναστάσεώς μου εἰς μαρτύριον, and tells us that Cyril of Jerusalem, in his fourth Homily, explains this passage in Zephaniah of the Martyrium, or Basilica, which Constantine built on the spot of the Lord's resurrection.

19. *Note to the 2009 edition:* See Book IV, note 12 above.

20. "The younger Constantine was appointed to hold his court in Gaul; and his brother Constantius exchanged that department, the ancient patrimony of their father, for the more opulent, but less martial, countries of the East. Italy, the Western Illyricum, and Africa,

were accustomed to revere Constans, the third of his sons, as the representative of the great Constantine." —Gibbon, *Decline and Fall*, chap. xviii.

21. In his *Chronicon*, Eusebius gives the more correct period of thirty years and ten months. Constantine's reign began AD 306 and his death took place AD 337.

22. These words seem to prove that the emperor now first became a catechumen.

23. It was customary for neophytes to wear white garments, which they laid aside on the eighth day from their baptism.

24. Alluding to his desire of being buried in the church of the Apostles, and sharing their honors, as noticed in Book IV, Chapter LVI, p. 201 of the present volume.

25. It appears that an interregnum of about three months took place, during which all laws and edicts continued to be issued in the name of Constantine, as before his death.

GENERAL INDEX

215

CPSIA information can be obtained at www.ICGtesting.com
Printed in the USA
BVOW08s1508150114

341777BV00001B/3/P